BRISTOL CATHEDRAL

History & Architecture

Dedication

Early fourteenth-century work at Bristol from the point of view of spatial imagination which is after all the architectural point of view par excellence – is superior to anything else built in England and indeed in Europe at the same time.
Sir Nikolaus Pevsner, 1958.

What matters at Bristol, however, is not the tracery patterns, but the three-dimensional spaces. For this is Europe's first Late Gothic 'hall church' with nave and aisles of equal height and continuous space — a type which in the fifteenth century became the progressive norm in Germany and Central Europe and, through German master-masons, in Spain.
Nicholas Taylor, 1968.

Whilst at Bristol I paid attention to the Cathedral in which I find many things deserving most particular attention. This cathedral has been generally overlooked . . . but the fact is there are parts about it equal to anything in the country.
A.W.N. Pugin to Mr Osmond, 1833.

BRISTOL CATHEDRAL

History & Architecture

Edited by John Rogan

TEMPUS

First published 2000

PUBLISHED IN THE UNITED KINGDOM BY:

Tempus Publishing Ltd
The Mill, Brimscombe Port
Stroud, Gloucestershire GL5 2QG

PUBLISHED IN THE UNITED STATES OF AMERICA BY:

Tempus Publishing Inc.
2A Cumberland Street
Charleston, SC 29401

Tempus books are available in France, Germany and Belgium
from the following addresses:

Tempus Publishing Group	Tempus Publishing Group	Tempus Publishing Group
21 Avenue de la République	Gustav-Adolf-Straße 3	Place de L'Alma 4/5
37300 Joué-lès-Tours	99084 Erfurt	1200 Brussels
FRANCE	GERMANY	BELGIUM

British Library Cataloguing in Publication Data.
A catalogue record for this book is available from the British Library.

ISBN 0 7524 1482 8

Typesetting and origination by Tempus Publishing.
PRINTED AND BOUND IN GREAT BRITAIN.

Contents

Acknowledgements

The authors and Friends of Bristol Cathedral gratefully acknowledge the following for permission to use illustrations:

Colour plates 1 – 5 photographs by English Life Publications Ltd

14 & **17** Bristol City Museum & Art Gallery

19 Sutton Publishing Ltd: William Barrett *The City and Antiquities of Bristol.* 1789, reprinted 1988

18, 23, 55 Thames & Hudson Ltd: G Cobb *English Cathedrals: the forgotten centuries.* 1980

Colour plate 15 Private collection

Colour plates 9 – 14, 16 – 21, Mr R H Moon

10, 11, 28, 29, 38 – 54 Mrs Sophie Johnson Church

Mrs J A Lawrence for preparing the text

Foreword

I am delighted to commend this book on the Abbey and Cathedral at Bristol. It makes a significant contribution to our appreciation of their history. The Cathedral Chapter wishes to record its warm appreciation of this labour of love.

The documentation of the art, architecture and history of cathedrals is becoming more and more important. Visitors to them are growing and they have increasing expectations about the quality of information given to them. Further, in an increasingly secular society an understanding of cathedrals is a significant way of presenting the Christian Gospel. If we understand the motivation of the builders we can go some way towards understanding their faith which lives on still, both in the building and the worshipping community.

We have benefited over the years from the scholarship of the Bristol and Gloucestershire Archaeological Society, the Bristol and Avon Archaeological Society, and the Bristol Branch of the Historical Association, as well as the Department of the History of Art in the University of Bristol. In particular, the untimely death of Dr M. Q. Smith has deprived us of much that was of great value. He made a major contribution to our appreciation of the buildings, and this book owes a great deal to his enthusiasm and expertise.

On behalf of the Chapter, I record our gratitude to the contributors and to the Friends of Bristol Cathedral who have carried the project through and underwritten its costs. We now have something substantial to place alongside the many valuable pamphlets which have been published over the years.

ROBERT GRIMLEY
Dean of Bristol

Feast of the Epiphany 2000

The illustrations

Colour plates

Text illustrations

Introduction

Bristol Cathedral is one of England's significant churches. It began life as an Augustinian abbey on an historic site. Since then much of the general history of England is evidenced in the history of the Abbey-Cathedral itself. College Green, the old graveyard, has as good a claim as any to be the place where St Augustine of the Papal Mission met St David, the leader of the old Romano-British Christians. The young Prince Henry, later Henry II, received much of his education here, in a region firmly loyal to his mother, the Empress Matilda, the daughter of Henry I. Once established as King, he showed himself to be a generous benefactor to the abbey which his officer, Robert Fitzharding, had established just over the river from the city and its castle. The Reformation made its way in the turbulence of the times, and the subsequent under-endowment of both the bishopric and the cathedral is a reminder of the financial problems which have bedevilled so much of church life.

The chapter and the cathedral were caught up in the trauma of the Civil Wars and the turmoil of the Revolution of 1688. The monuments bear witness to the economic expansion of England but with silence about the slave trade. Canon Sydney Smith preached the cause of Catholic Emancipation from the pulpit. The mob vented its fury upon the Bishop's Palace and the Cathedral chapter in its frustration at the failure of the Reform Bill. The work of Canon Barnett educated the middle classes in the needs of the new industrial working classes, both here and at Toynbee Hall; and Canon Hakluyt chronicled the exploits of Elizabethan seamen. There are monuments to the greater and lesser wars in which the nation was involved. The building itself was damaged during the 1939–45 war, and those who gave war service in the city are commemorated in the windows.

Ecclesiastically, the Harrowing of Hell stone bears witness to the practice of the Christian faith at the time of the first millennium. The vitality of the Victorines in the Augustinian Order is displayed in their scandal-free history. The tensions between the church and the public authorities, both nationally and locally, occur in the Cathedral's history. Bishop Joseph Butler, one of England's greatest philosophic theologians, served longer in Bristol than he did in Durham and his pointed exchange with the Rev John Wesley went to the heart of vocation and ministry. Bishop Newton's writings identify serious weaknesses in the life of the church which were to be rectified by vigorous reform in the nineteenth century, which transformed the constitution and life of cathedrals. The rising civic sense and general awareness of the need for adequate church provision is exemplified in the programme which led to the rebuilding of the nave, for which the church had waited for so many centuries.

Like many other cathedrals, Bristol bears witness to the richness of the Anglican choral tradition, but architecturally it possesses important examples of Romanesque architecture, while the hall church design is of European significance. The Victorian Gothic of the western part of the building is particularly good. A sympathetic appreciation of this style has been slow to come; few churches in England are free of its variable influence. Here the genius of Street has produced something creative, encouraging the critic to take a more favourable view of both the idiom and, indeed, the Cathedral as a whole. For as Pugin commented, the building has been overlooked but contains things which are the equal of anything in the country. In this book we introduce them to the reader.

Note on contributors

Dr Joseph H. Bettey was formerly Reader in Local History at the University of Bristol
Dr Catherine Oakes is Lecturer in the History of Art at the University of Bristol
Canon John Rogan M.A., B.Phil. is the Cathedral Archivist
Mr Alan M. Rome O.B.E., F.R.I.B.A., F.S.A. is the Cathedral Architect

1 St Augustine's Abbey 1140-1539

The Augustinian abbey which was later to become Bristol Cathedral was founded by Robert Fitzharding in 1140. Fitzharding was a member of a long-established West-Country family which had survived the Norman Conquest and had become major landowners in Bristol and the surrounding region. An early sixteenth-century inscription which survives on the north side of the abbey gatehouse describes Robert Fitzharding as a descendant of the King of Denmark, but this seems to be an attempt by the Augustinian canons to enhance the status of their founder. All the evidence suggests that he was the son of an English thegn named Alnod or Ethnothus. Fitzharding evidently profited from the lively sea-borne trade and commerce of Bristol, and he steered an astute course through the bloody upheavals of the civil war that followed the death of Henry I in 1135. In this war, Bristol, with its castle, was one of the major strongholds of Matilda, and Fitzharding was rewarded for his loyalty to her cause with further grants of land. Eventually he was awarded the lordship of Berkeley, which had formerly been held by Stephen's supporter, Roger of Berkeley, who paid the penalty for his loyalty to the losing side in the war. The connection between Fitzharding's descendants as lords of Berkeley and the Augustinian abbey at Bristol was to remain important throughout the Middle Ages.

Fitzharding continued in the royal favour after the accession of Matilda's son as Henry II in 1154. Henry had spent part of his boyhood at Bristol castle, and evidently remembered his time there with affection. When he became King he granted a charter to Bristol in 1155, and greatly augmented the endowments of the abbey. His name still appears as joint founder with Fitzharding on the later abbey gatehouse, although the abbey never laid claim to being a royal foundation. The part played by Henry II in the foundation of the abbey is best summed up by a phrase in a charter granted by Robert Fitzharding in 1159. This confirms his gifts of lands and property to the canons. In the charter he described the abbey which 'by the grace of God and by the help of my lord the king I have founded' *(per gratiam dei et per auxilium domini mei regis ecclesiam fundavi)*. Robert Fitzharding's extensive properties included the Manor of Billeswick across the river Frome and beyond the town defences of Bristol. Here he founded his monastery for Augustinian canons in 1140, and dedicated it to St Augustine, the apostle of the English.

There has been much discussion about the site of the abbey, its relationship with the church of St Augustine the Less a short distance to the east, the links with the cult of St Jordan and with the remarkable pre-Conquest carving of the Harrowing of Hell, which is now displayed in the south transept of the cathedral. The records are scanty and uncertain, but it seems probable that a church on the site of St Augustine the Less was already in existence when the abbey was founded in 1140, and may have been used for their services by the earliest canons whilst the church of the new abbey was being built. Most of the archaeological evidence concerning the early history of St Augustine the Less was destroyed when the church was rebuilt in 1480. It was finally demolished in 1962 after extensive damage by bombs in 1940. Excavations on the site, however, revealed the foundations of an eleventh-century church, together with burials of that period. There was a late-medieval tradition in Bristol that St Jordan was one of the monks who accompanied St Augustine when he met with the British Christians somewhere along the Severn in 603, and that he died and was buried in Bristol. There was certainly a chapel dedicated to St Jordan on College Green throughout the later Middle Ages, and it is mentioned in the fifteenth-century account rolls of the abbey.

Writing in c.1540, John Leland refers to 'A chapel in which St Jordan, the disciple of St Augustine apostle of the English, is buried'. In c.1580 William Camden in his *Britannia* described College Green and 'a pulpit of stone and a chapel wherein they say Jordan, companion to St Austin the English apostle was buried'. The building on College Green is clearly marked on Jacob Millerd's detailed map of Bristol made in 1673, but by that time it was being used for secular purposes. Sadly, all evidence of the chapel was destroyed when the surface of College Green was lowered during construction of the Council House in the 1950s. Further confirmation for the cult of St Jordan comes from the fact that the unusual Christian name, Jordan, was in use in Bristol during the early Middle Ages, and one of Robert Fitzharding's sons bore that name.

The strongest evidence of all for an earlier religious building on or near the site of St Augustine's abbey is the massive carving, 7ft (1.7m) in height, depicting the 'Harrowing of Hell' which is now displayed in the south transept of the cathedral. It dates from c.1000–1050 and shows the powerful figure of the risen Christ treading upon the devil and drawing up two naked figures out of the depths of Hell. This remarkable carving was discovered beneath the floor of the cathedral chapter house during repairs in 1836. Although there is no conclusive proof, all the evidence points to the fact that the place chosen by Robert Fitzharding for his new monastery was already the site of a religious cult linked to St Augustine of Canterbury and his companion, St Jordan.

Fitzharding founded his abbey for Augustinian canons who followed the Rule first set down in the fifth century by St Augustine of Hippo. By the twelfth century the Augustinians had replaced the Benedictines as the monastic order most frequently chosen by wealthy and pious individuals who were founding new monasteries, and the Bristol canons were part of the strict Victorine section of their order, owing allegiance to the highly-respected house of St Victor in Paris. The Augustinians were known as the Black Canons from their monastic dress of long black cassock and hood. They were priests who had taken monastic vows and lived a communal life. Their primary duty was the celebration of masses and the maintenance of a regular, daily round of services. The first canons to arrive at Bristol came from the recently-founded Victorine house which began at Shobdon in Herefordshire and later moved to Wigmore in the same county. The earliest canons at Shobdon had come from St Victor in Paris, and the first abbot at Bristol, Richard of Warwick, had been at St Victor and later at Shobdon.

Following the formal foundation of the abbey in 1140, there was an inevitable delay while suitable buildings were erected for the accommodation of the canons, and a church was built in which they could maintain a regular round of worship. There is some doubt over the precise chronology since most of the surviving sources date from many years later and are inconsistent. It seems likely, however, that by 1148 work was sufficiently advanced for the abbey church to be dedicated, and in that year the first six canons were formally installed. This is based on the evidence of the Roll or chronicle of the history of the abbey compiled by Abbot John Newland, who was abbot from 1481 until his death in 1515. This chronicle was preserved among the Berkeley family archives at Berkeley castle, and is a major source of information about the abbey and its successive abbots.

Newland's Roll describes the course of events at the foundation of the abbey as follows:

> This goode lorde (Robert Fitzharding) primere fundator and Chanon of the Monastery of Seint Augustines bi Bristowe began the fundacion of the same in the yere of our Lord MCXL. And bilded the churche and all other howses of offices according to the same bi the space of vi yeres

Robert Fitzharding is described not only as founder (fundator) but also as a canon (Chanon) of the monastery because for a few years before his death in 1170 he entered the abbey and became an Augustinian canon. On his death he was buried in the abbey church at the entrance to the choir, between the stalls of the abbot and the prior. His wife, Eva, became the first abbess of the small Augustinian nunnery of St Mary Magdalen, which the Fitzhardings had founded on the slopes of St Michael's Hill, overlooking Bristol. Abbot Newland's Roll also describes St Augustine's abbey as 'bi (by) Bristowe', and throughout the Middle Ages the abbey was referred to as juxta (next to) Bristol or 'without Bristol'. This recognised the fact that it was outside the medieval walls of the town and on the western side of the river Frome.

Fitzharding's wealth enabled him to endow his abbey with numerous estates, properties and churches, especially in Bristol and the surrounding region. As a result of his bequests and of further endowments given by other members of his family and by King Henry II, the abbey soon became wealthy and influential. Throughout the Middle Ages it remained the richest and most important ecclesiastical institution in Bristol. Detailed information about the abbey's possessions has been made available in Canon David Walker's skilful edition of the abbey Cartulary or list of charters, revealing all the donors and details of their gifts which was compiled in 1270. As well as numerous parish churches that were 'appropriated' by the abbey and from which it drew a major part of the tithes, there were widespread estates in Somerset and Gloucestershire.

In Somerset the canons possessed lands at Abbots Leigh, Leigh Woods, Portbury, Ham Green, Failand, Wraxall, Portishead, Clevedon, Weston-super-Mare, Tickenham, Weare and Pawlett. Elsewhere in Somerset they drew rents from Rowberrow, Blagdon, East and West Harptree, Baggridge and Farmborough. The Gloucestershire estates stretched along the Severn and included Horfield, Filton, the valuable manor of Almondsbury, Hill, Cromhall, Berkeley and Slimbridge. The canons' ownership of Arlington is still remembered in the name of St Augustine's farm at the centre of the village, and their ownership of the rich manor of Ashleworth on the Severn, north of Gloucester, is evident

1-3 Decorations from 1350
     Temporale

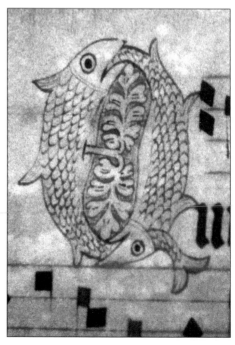

from the late-medieval manorhouse and splendid barn which survives there. Other Gloucestershire properties given to the Augustinians of Bristol included the manors of Codrington and Wapley, part of the manor of Wotton-under-Edge, and land at South Cerney. Further afield they derived a regular income from the tithes of the parish churches at Finmere in Oxfordshire, Halberton in Devon, from lands at Fifehead Magdalen in Dorset, and from churches and estates in Wales and Ireland.

With such large endowments and the regular income they provided, the canons could afford to press ahead with the construction of the monastic church, together with the cloister, chapter house, dormitory, 'frater' or dining room, and other buildings. A charter of *c.*1159 records the gift by Robert Fitzharding of land at Horfield when the canons entered their new church. An early seal of the abbey shows that the church consisted of a small chancel, two transepts and a nave of six bays. The quality of the work that the abbey could afford, even at this early stage of its development, is evident from the superb architecture of the chapter house, which remains the finest Romanesque building of its kind in the country, and in the two surviving gateways with their fine Romanesque carving. The size and shape of the nave at the Norman abbey church were confirmed in 1869 when the architect, G.E. Street, was engaged in building a new nave for the cathedral. He reported that in digging the foundations the workmen had quickly come to the solid rock on which the building stands. In addition, they had found 'considerable portions of the foundations of the old Norman Nave'. Street traced the foundations of this continuous wall, and found it to be 109ft in length by 29ft 6in in width, with walls 5ft 9in thick. He also discovered the foundations of a cloister on the south side of the nave which was 10ft 6in in width.

As with most monasteries, the history of St Augustine's is largely known through the succession of abbots on whom the success of the house depended. It was their ability, sanctity of life, conduct of affairs and political skill that ensured the reputation of the house and brought continuing bequests. Most of the canons remain as shadowy figures, only appearing in the surviving records when admonished for some fault or when involved in some scandalous conduct. Sadly, the conscientious performance of duties and careful observance of the abbey's central function of maintaining prayer and praise to the Almighty never merit any mention. The first abbot, Richard of Warwick, was clearly an impressive and energetic figure. Having been chosen by Robert Fitzharding to preside over the launch of the new abbey in 1148, he remained as abbot until his death in 1177. During this period the abbey was successfully established, many endowments were obtained, and major building work was completed, including the first abbey church and the still-surviving chapter house and vestibule with their fine architecture. Richard's successor, William of Saltmarsh, came from the Berkeley estates in the Severn valley, and he had served as chamberlain and possibly as prior of St Augustine's abbey. He was abbot from 1177 until 1186 when he became bishop of Llandaff. The next abbot, John, held office for thirty years from 1186 until 1216. During this time the abbey received many further gifts and endowments, and building work continued on the cloisters and domestic buildings, but we know nothing of the abbot himself.

Much more is known about his successor, Abbot David (1216-34). He was active in promoting the interests of the abbey in every way, and maintained contacts with other

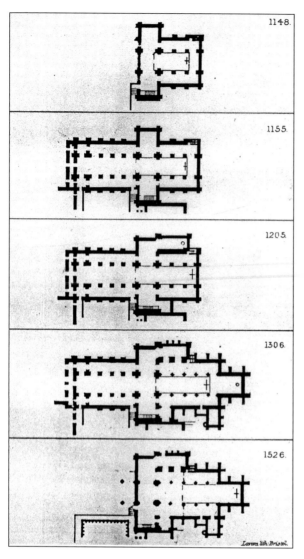

4   Development of the abbey

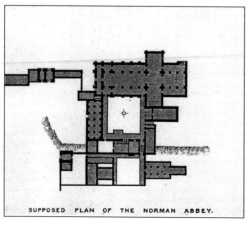

SUPPOSED PLAN OF THE NORMAN ABBEY.

5   Plan of the Norman abbey

6 *Plan from William de*
   Wyrcestre

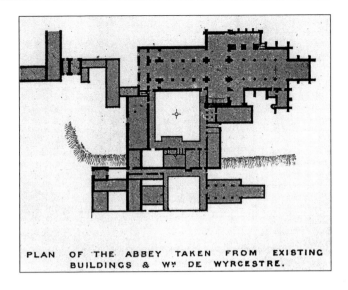

PLAN OF THE ABBEY TAKEN FROM EXISTING
BUILDINGS & Wᵐ DE WYRCESTRE.

Augustinian abbots, powerful national figures and local gentry. His energy and commitment seem to have brought him into conflict with his canons: his period of office was marked by disputes, and he appears to have resigned or been deposed in 1234. He remained at the abbey until his death in 1253. Our knowledge of Abbot David rests on the survival of copies of 46 letters written by him during the period 1218-22. Many of the letters deal with the routine business of the abbey and the management of its estates; others are concerned with the links between Augustinian abbots in England and the mother house of St Victor in Paris. In a letter to the bishop of Exeter, Abbot David arranges for the body of a member of the Berkeley family to be brought to St Augustine's for burial, and so that 'by constant remembrance of the deceased, the devotion of the living may increase, and there may be more plentiful almsgiving and offering of prayers for the common solace of the dead'. He adds that most other members of the Berkeley family are buried in the abbey. Several of the letters deal with the difficulties of managing the estates that the abbey had been given around Kilkenny in Ireland. They show that in 1218 Abbot David sailed to Wexford and visited the Irish possessions. An indication of his character is revealed in his ironic conclusion that the problem of the Irish properties was so complex that it could only be resolved by divine intervention. Many later abbots were to echo this weary verdict.

By far the most remarkable achievement of Abbot David was the construction of what was later to be known as the Elder Lady Chapel. This was originally constructed as a separate building, entered from the north transept of the abbey; later, the extension of the chancel incorporated the south wall. With its elegant proportions and lively carvings the chapel remains one of the most attractive features of the whole building. The similarities with the contemporary workmanship and carvings at Wells cathedral are obvious, and remarkably the connection can be well authenticated. Among Abbot David's letters is one to the Dean of Wells asking him to lend his stone-carver ('your servant L') from Wells to work on the new Lady Chapel at Bristol. This almost certainly refers to Adam Lock, who was the master mason at Wells up to 1229, and whose work at Wells has numerous parallels with that at Bristol. Small fragments of paint and traces of colour on some of the walls of the Elder Lady Chapel bear witness to the fact that it was once bright with colour, much like the present Eastern Lady Chapel. An elaborately illustrated and decorated psalter from the early thirteenth century also survives. This psalter is now in Czechoslovakia, but was made for use in St Augustine's and was possibly the gift of a canon who is shown kneeling beneath a scroll, giving his name as Frater Robertus. The decoration of the psalter matches that of the Elder Lady Chapel, with foliage, animals, monsters and human figures. It provides an indication of the rich and colourful possessions with which the abbey was furnished.

Many years later, Abbot Newland's Roll recorded that when Abbot David died he was 'beried under a Marble Stone with a hedde and a Cross made of the same in the Elder Chapelle of our Lady the yere of our Lord MCCLIII'. This now badly-decayed memorial slab of Purbeck marble survives on the floor of the north transept by the entrance to the Lady Chapel. The Bristol historian, Samuel Seyer, writing in 1826 described the stone as 'still tolerably perfect, lying at the entrance to the chapel'.

Abbot David's period of office witnessed the establishment of a generously-endowed hospital by Maurice de Gaunt, grandson of Robert Fitzharding, in what had been the abbey almonry. This was situated to the north of the abbey and later became known as St Mark's Hospital or the Gaunts. According to the original charter, the hospital's work of feeding the poor was to be supervised by the prior of the abbey. After Maurice de Gaunt died in 1230, his nephew, Robert de Gournay, provided further endowments. At the same time, Maurice's younger brother, Henry de Gaunt, was appointed as head of the hospital, which now became separate from St Augustine's abbey. A new constitution provided for a master, six chaplains, six clerks and five lay brothers, while the obligation of feeding the poor was reduced from 100 to 27 paupers each day. St Augustine's abbey was now faced with a well-endowed, independent establishment on the edge of its precinct, and the two institutions were to be frequently in conflict with each other during the next three centuries.

Like many other monastic institutions, St Augustine's fluctuated between periods of austerity when the Rule was carefully observed, the endowments were profitably managed and the buildings were well maintained, and periods when human weakness and the inevitable tedium and tensions of monastic life led to slackness, indiscipline and neglect. Little evidence survives concerning the daily life in the abbey or of the regular round of services. Most of our detailed knowledge comes from the records of episcopal visitations. By their nature such enquiries were concerned with finding faults and correcting abuses, so that they provide an unbalanced picture, but they are almost all the evidence we have. Until the establishment of a Bristol diocese in 1542, Bristol north of the Avon was part of the large diocese of Worcester, and periodic visitations to the abbey were conducted by the bishops of Worcester or their representatives.

In 1251 a visitation by the bishop of Worcester revealed that relations between the abbey and the Gaunt's Hospital had already deteriorated badly. The dispute involved the monastic precinct, later to be known as College Green. This pleasant green space was used by both institutions for access and as a burial ground. It also contained St Jordan's chapel and an open-air pulpit or preaching cross. The bishop ordered that the brethren of the

Hospital should acknowledge the rights of St Augustine's over the whole green, that the abbot had the right to cut the grass for use on the floors of the abbey, and of St Augustine the Less. Both houses could continue to bury their dead there, but the ground should be kept level and not heaped up over the graves 'in order to preserve the pleasantness of the place'. This sensible decision failed to produce harmony, and bickering between the two neighbours continued.

Much more serious faults were recorded in 1278 after a visitation by the energetic bishop Godfrey Giffard. He found that the abbot, John de Marina, was ineffective and ill-educated; the canons were indisciplined; the buildings were neglected; the services performed in a slovenly manner; and 'the house is not well ruled in temporal matters, for none of the brethren know what they have nor what they spend'. The bishop imposed a long list of injunctions aimed at reforming the low standards. His orders included the maintenance of silence in church, cloister and refectory, an end to canons wandering about the town, no more drinking sessions in the infirmary, more regular charity, the discipline of ill-behaved canons and better management of the estates. Above all, the regular services were to be performed in a more dignified manner. The canons were ordered not 'to fly out of the choir like bees' as soon as services were ended, but to remain and pray for their benefactors.

When the bishop came again in 1284 he found that all was well. Yet a year later the Patent Rolls record of King Edward I ordered the constable of Bristol to supervise the abbey estate management and curtail the expenses because the debts of the abbey were so great. Nonetheless, in spite of its shortcomings, the abbey continued to attract gifts and endowments. In particular, the Berkeley family remained generous benefactors, and members of the family continued to be buried in the abbey church. By the end of the thirteenth century the increasing wealth of the abbey enabled the tenth abbot, Edmund Knowle, to begin a major reconstruction of the abbey church. Knowle was one of the greatest of the abbots, and his re-building of the chancel provided the abbey church with a significant place in architectural history as an early example of a hall church built to a new and adventurous design. Knowle was abbot 1306-1332, but the work to replace the small Norman chancel may have begun while he was treasurer of the abbey from 1298. As well as the chancel, the cloisters, the frater or dining room, and a building at the west end of the church known as the Camera Regia or King's Chamber used to accommodate important guests, were also re-built during Knowle's abbacy. The work was so important that two centuries later Newland's Roll was able to state the precise hour at which building commenced, recording that Abbot Knowle 'began that grete werke the sixth day after the Assumption of our Lady (August 21) at the oure (hour) of ix, the yere of our Lord mciiii xx xviii (1298)'.

Inevitably with such large building projects, work continued for many years at vast expense. No doubt it was difficult to maintain an ordered religious life in the midst of so much work involving so many labourers. It was partly the increase in the number of canons to more than 20 which made it necessary to provide additional altars where all might say Mass. Thus the new wider chancel had a Lady Chapel at its east end, and also joined the Elder Lady Chapel to the north. On the south the Newton and Berkeley chapels also provided space for more altars. The continuing patronage of the Berkeley

7   Depiction of Crucifixion from Missal of 1450

8   *Page of 1450 Missal. Feast of St Margaret and St Mary Magdalene*

9 *Page of 1450 Missal. First Mass of the Nativity*

family is evident from the heraldry in the new work and by a series of distinctive 'stellate' tomb-recesses. The Berkeley chapel must have been completed soon after 1321 since Thomas, Lord Berkeley, who died in that year, is buried with his wife Joan (died 1309), under an arch between the chapel and the south choir aisle. Building work continued under Knowle's successor, Abbot John Snow, and can be dated by another Berkeley burial. Margaret, Lady Berkeley, who died in 1337, is buried under an arch in the wall, the wall which joins the Elder Lady Chapel to the north choir aisle. Later, her son Lord Maurice Berkeley, who died in 1368, was buried beside her.

Abbot Knowle's enthusiasm for his numerous building projects may have been at the expense of a strictly disciplined life within the abbey. In 1307 there was a major conflict with the Prior of Worcester who attempted to conduct a visitation to the abbey on behalf of the bishop. The Prior and his retinue were refused admission by the abbey porter and were forced to lodge at an inn in Bristol. Although one of the canons, John Rogan, was sent to discuss matters with the Prior, no agreement was reached and the Prior was forced to depart. Later, episcopal visitations revealed that the canons were impoverished and short of food because of expenditure on building work, that there was considerable laxity in behaviour and that the abbot and the canons shared a common passion for hunting and kept many hounds. In 1320 it was reported that services were badly conducted and that an insufficient number of canons attended. One canon, William Barry, sowed discord among his brethren; another canon, Henry of Gloucester, did not carry out his duty of distributing alms regularly; and John of Shaftesbury was said to consort with an unknown woman. In 1331 Abbot Knowle was obliged to seek a pardon from King Edward III for having been found hunting in the King's park at Clarendon near Salisbury. Remarkably, the abbot seems to have selected the apparently disreputable John of Shaftesbury as his companion on this expedition.

In 1340 another visitation revealed a long list of faults, but the bishop, Wolstan de Bransford, was lenient in the injunctions he imposed. The bishop had been a monk himself and no doubt realised the difficulty of maintaining high standards year after year. He therefore gently ordered that disputes between canons should cease, that conversation should always be in French or Latin, that alms were to be regularly distributed and that all the services should be well attended. To soften his blows even further, the bishop accompanied each exhortation by long extracts from the bible.

As a crowded, busy and no doubt insanitary port, visited by many foreign ships and attracting people from all over the West Country, Bristol was badly affected by the Black Death of 1348-9, and by subsequent outbreaks of the plague. Before the plague there were 25 canons at St Augustine's, but during 1348-9 the number dropped to 15. Losses from the plague were soon replaced, but numbers were never again to exceed 18, although they remained stable at that level until the Dissolution. The income of the abbey was affected by the death of tenants in the plague epidemic and by the changed economic circumstances thereafter. There were several complaints about debts and financial problems during the later fourteenth century and warnings over the need to avoid excessive expense.

One apparently unavoidable expense which the abbey was forced to endure was the necessity of providing maintenance for various royal retainers who were sent to the abbey to live out the rest of their lives in comfort. One of many examples occurred in 1351 when the royal servant, William of Rical, was sent to Bristol by Edward III with an order that he should be maintained at St Augustine's in the same manner as William Alfret, another royal servant now deceased. Some abbots were also guilty of excessive expenditure, both on the abbot's lodging at Bristol and in the manor house at Leigh (Abbots Leigh). In 1366 there were complaints that the abbey was sheltering people of ill-fame, that it was mismanaging its estates by granting unprofitable leases, and that Abbot Henry Shalingford was profligate and the abbey was much in debt because of 'the excessive and unproductive expenses of the said Henry'. During the next few years there were several other references to the misrule of Abbot Henry.

In 1374, while the bishopric of Worcester was vacant, a visitation of St Augustine's abbey was conducted by the Prior of Worcester. He found much to criticise and left a long list of orders to regulate future conduct and settle disputes between the abbot and the canons. Seven trustworthy canons were to join with the abbot in taking all-important decisions, to have custody of the common seal and to supervise sales of corn from the estates. The services were to be maintained 'as was accustomed of old time'. Better food was to be provided for the canons, and they were to be allowed suitable recreation after dinner 'in due place as time allows'. Above all, 'peace, love and quiet' were to be restored within the abbey.

It is not known how canons were chosen for the abbey, but it is evident from their names that many came from the West Country. For example, in 1352, when Abbot Ralph de Asshe died, a meeting of the canons was held in the chapter house to elect a successor. In the aftermath of the Black Death there were only seventeen canons, but among them were Robert Dunster, Simon de Tormarton, Robert de Syde, John Badminton, Walter Cheltenham, Laurence de Cirencestre, John de Launston, Thomas de Bykenore and Walter de Shaftesbury. They elected William Cok or Coke who had been the sub-prior as abbot. A rare glimpse of the way in which the atmosphere of a medieval monastery differed from modern notions of appropriate behaviour in church is provided by an entry in the episcopal register of Worcester recording the election of William Coke in 1352. This describes how the canons had assembled in the chapter house for the election of a new abbot, and that nine had voted for William Coke and eight for various other candidates. The Prior, Robert de Syde, announced the result:

'Whereupon, all having approved of the election,
they raised the said William in their hands from
the ground and carried him to the high altar, singing
Te Deum Laudamus, and laid him upon the same
altar, as is the custom'.

Most of the service books of the abbey were destroyed at the Reformation, but in addition to the thirteenth-century psalter that was mentioned earlier, fragments of a service book survive from the fourteenth century. This consists of 16 pages from a Temporale or choir book containing words and music sung at the Mass during the regular course of the seasons. These pages escaped destruction because they were used as wrappers for the accounts of the cathedral, established in 1542 after the suppression of the abbey in 1539. The pages contain the beautifully-written text in red and black letters, together with the elaborate musical notation for the sung parts of the Mass. A charming feature of these pages is that the initial letters are decorated with numerous grotesques and fantastic creatures, including a dog biting a monster, a merman with a bow, a fish with a dagger, a dragon and a snake. The mass for St Stephen's day shows an evil-looking man about to throw a stone, while another shows an Augustinian canon using a buckler to repel an arrow while brandishing a curry-comb in his other hand. The colourful pages provide a reminder that the central purpose of the abbey was the daily round of services, and that these continued despite plague, building work, debt or scandal.

An unusual problem was revealed in a visitation by the Archbishop of Canterbury, William Courtenay, in 1384. He complained that the canons wore high boots of black

10 Staircase to Treasury

leather which had to be kept oiled or greased. In consequence the white vestments at the altar were made filthy and disreputable, 'so dirty as to be a scandal to beholders'. The archbishop ordered that they were to wear cloth leggings 'in price not more than 20d per yard', but that they could wear boots when outside the monastery. One canon, Adam Horsley, was severely criticised for his conduct since he had 'badly administered and wasted the goods of the monastery'. Evidently he was a difficult and disruptive person, and shortly afterwards he was sent to Ireland to supervise the management of the abbey properties. In spite of all criticisms, however, the abbey remained an important, wealthy and prestigious institution. Its status was confirmed in 1398 when Pope Boniface IX granted to the abbot, John Daubeny, and his successors the coveted right to wear a mitre and other episcopal insignia, thereby recognising it as one of the major English religious houses.

As landowners concerned to receive the maximum return from their property, the Augustinian canons were unlikely to be popular. In Bristol they never shared in the popular esteem enjoyed by the friars, and were perceived as outside and remote from Bristol and its people. There were several occasions of violent protest against the actions of the canons as landlords. One fruitful cause of dispute in Bristol was the abbey's ownership of Treen Mill on the Malago Brook, close to where it joined the Avon downstream from St Mary Redcliffe, on a site now occupied by Bathurst Basin. The mill, which was no doubt called Treen because of its wooden construction, was part of the endowment received from the Berkeleys. As early as 1220 Abbot David was involved in a dispute with Bristol townsfolk over rights at the mill and at the ferry that plied across the Avon at that point. Subsequently, there are numerous references to complaints about the mill, and in 1399 there were major disturbances led by the mayor, John Canynge, when the mill and its watercourses were damaged and the townsmen 'seized and imprisoned and threatened the canons and servants of the abbot in life and limb and daily continue other oppressions'. Even more violent protests occurred in 1468 when the abbey was obliged to spend £120 re-building four mills 'called Trynemills near the cliffs called Redcliff' which had been badly damaged by the protestors. From time to time there were also violent protests against the abbey's management of its rural estates. There were riots at Leigh (Abbots Leigh) in 1325 and occasional violent protests against various features of abbey policy elsewhere. In 1452 a large number of men from the abbey properties in north Somerset and south Gloucestershire arrived in Bristol, broke into the abbot's house and assaulted him there.

The most serious quarrel between the abbey and the town of Bristol occurred in the period 1491-1496. The climax was an armed conflict on St Augustine's Green in 1496. The dispute concerned the abbey's claim of complete jurisdiction over its own extensive precinct, including the green now known as College Green. Further sources of conflict arose over the right of the abbey to grant unlimited sanctuary to criminals fleeing from justice. These matters had been fruitful causes of dispute for many years. In June 1496 matters came to a head when the mayor, William Regent, and his officials were accompanied by numerous townsfolk and made a procession to St Augustine's Green to assert their rights, and to conduct an 'Assize of Bread' — that is to examine the quality and weight of the loaves of bread baked within the abbey precinct. They were confronted by the abbey constable, officials and servants who, it was alleged, fell upon the mayor's procession with poleaxes, staves and bills, while one of the canons arrived wielding a halberd. Meanwhile the mayor's men were said to have broken into some of the houses around the Green, and violent struggles ensued. The mayor attempted to calm matters by shouting 'Keep the Peace' until he was hoarse. Eventually Abbot John Newland appeared and a meeting was arranged between the parties in front of St Mark's Hospital. The abbot handed over an Irishman — who had been sentenced in the Mayor's court and then fled to the abbey for sanctuary — to the mayor for trial. Thereafter mayor and abbot jointly weighed bread together on the Green.

The whole dispute, which had dragged on for many years, was only settled through the mediation of Cardinal Morton, Archbishop of Canterbury, and the Lord Chief Justice, although many of the issues remained unresolved. This illustrates the tensions that had built up over rights of jurisdiction, irritation at sanctuary granted to fugitives from justice, frustration at the abbey's ownership of mills which competed with the corporation's own mills, and a host of minor disagreements. It also illustrates the growing confidence of the mayor and corporation of Bristol and their lack of respect or support for the remote figures of the abbot and canons of St Augustine's. When making their wills late-medieval Bristolians made generous bequests to their parish churches, to the four Bristol friaries and to local hospitals and almshouses; they even made token gifts of small sums to the cathedral at far-away Worcester, and for parishioners south of the Avon, to the cathedral at Wells. But few left anything to St Augustine's which remained irrelevant to them. When the final reckoning came under Henry VIII the Augustinian monks had few supporters in Bristol.

Meanwhile, in the early fifteenth century, the large annual income of the abbey

11 Night stairs

enabled the canons to resume the major building work that had been suspended following the catastrophe of the Black Death. It was during the long abbacy of Walter Newbury from 1428 to 1473 that many new buildings were erected or existing ones extended. Newbury's period of office was interrupted for five years (1451-56) when, for reasons which remain unclear, he was deposed by the canons, and Thomas Sutton was elected as abbot in his place. By 1456, however, Sutton had become so unpopular that he was accused of wasting the resources of the abbey and was himself deposed. Walter Newbury was then restored as abbot, and continued until his death in 1473. Abbot Newbury was responsible for several building projects on the abbey estates, notably at Fifehead Magdalen in Dorset, Leigh (Abbots Leigh) in Somerset and Almondsbury in Gloucestershire. Most impressive of all is his surviving work on the abbey estate at Ashleworth, on the banks of the Severn north of Gloucester. Under Abbot Newbury Ashleworth parish church was substantially re-built, and a new manor house and manorial court house were constructed. Later, under Abbot John Newland, a large new barn was provided to store the produce of the abbey lands. This whole complex of fine buildings at Ashleworth remains a remarkable memorial to the work of the two great abbots.

It was during the abbacy of Walter Newbury that a beautifully-illuminated missal was

12 Abbey gate house and Old Deanery

made for use on the high altar of the abbey. This missal has survived and is one of the treasures of Bristol Reference Library. It is a superb example of late-medieval calligraphy and book production. The highly-decorated pages, elegant text and musical notation give an indication of the elaborate services and rich furnishings of the abbey church.

Abbot Newbury was also responsible for major building work on the abbey church. This included the construction of a large, new central tower equipped with bells, and re-construction of the transepts. Work on the transepts with fine, ribbed vaulting and interesting carved bosses was continued under Abbot William Hunt (1473-81), and during the long rule and forceful leadership of Abbot John Newland (1481-1515). The recumbent effigies of these three abbots, Newbury, Hunt and Newland, are in the early fourteenth-century niches in the walls of the Eastern Lady Chapel.

Abbot Newland, who was also known as Nailheart from his rebus or badge of a heart pierced by three nails, deserves to take his place with Abbot Edmund Knowle as one of the greatest of the abbots. Both were notable builders, and a great deal of their work survives. Abbot Newland was an efficient administrator, devoting himself to the astute management of the abbey's resources in order to finance the building work. He kept the offices of treasurer and cellarer in his own hands, and the surviving accounts show that the financial affairs of the abbey were in good order. Building work during his abbacy included numerous churches, houses and barns on the abbey estates, including five new

13 Entrance to the medieval choir

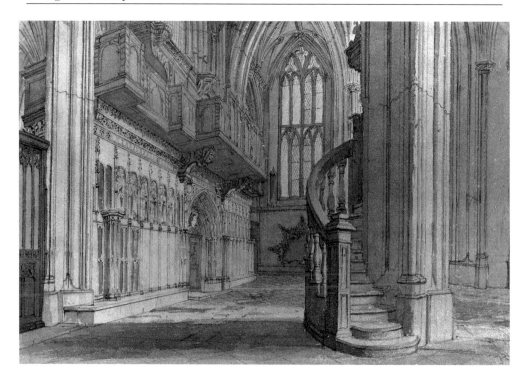

14 The medieval pulpitum

barns in the parish of Berkeley, and the fine barn that survives at Ashleworth. At the abbey itself, the abbey church consisted of the large chancel and Lady Chapel, which had been built during the early fourteenth century, and the small low Romanesque nave, which was known as the 'old church' and was quite out of scale with the chancel. Newland began the major work of replacing this nave. Because the new nave was to be longer and wider than the old, work could start on the new walls while leaving the existing nave undisturbed. By the time of Newland's death in 1515, the foundations had been laid and the new walls on the north and west sides had reached to the sills of the windows. Abbot Newland was also responsible for re-building the cloisters, the upper part of the gatehouse, the dormitory, frater or dining room and the prior's lodging. In many parts of the surviving buildings his rebus of the heart and nails can still be seen. A list compiled in 1498 gives the names of Abbot Newland and twenty canons.

In 1480 William Worcestre (1415-85), who had been born in Bristol, compiled his detailed description of the town, complete with measurements of its churches, streets, lanes and quays. He described 'the Liberty of St Augustine's abbey precinct', with the church of St Augustine the Less 'rebuilt this year of Christ 1480'. He suggested that the site of St Augustine the Less was where 'the old original church of the said abbey' once stood. He lists the household buildings of the abbey, including the granary, bakehouse, brewhouse and stables, and gives the measurements of the abbey church. There was a great contrast between the splendid chancel, Lady Chapel, side chapels and tower of the abbey church, and the old low Norman nave. The disparity between the two parts of the church must have given it an odd appearance. Worcestre gave the dimensions of the quire as 64 steps in length and 50 wide; the nave, which he described as 'the old church', measured 80 steps by 64. He also paced the measurements of the Chapter House and of the canons' frater or dining room.

Newland was succeeded as abbot by Robert Elyot (1515-25), William Burton (1525-39) and Morgan ap Gwilliam (1539). Abbot Elyot was responsible for the choir stalls, many of which still bear his initials. The stalls are notable for the lively carvings of the misericords beneath the seats, with scenes from daily life and from popular fables such as 'the Romance of Reynard the Fox'. Since misericords were out of sight under the canons' seats in the choir, carvers could depict all sorts of secular, and often explicitly bawdy, scenes. The Bristol carvings also illustrate the new early-Renaissance fashions and motifs. In the Victorian period a few of them were thought to be so obscene that they were destroyed. As well as the Reynard the Fox stories, other subjects include nude wrestlers, nude boys chased by a two-headed dragon, a mermaid with monsters, a woman beating a man, men with a bear in a wheelbarrow, men whipping a slug or snail carrying a burden, a stag and hounds, apes and exotic beasts, all surrounded by flowers and foliage inhabited by human faces or animals.

During William Burton's abbacy the elaborately-crested parapet was added above the reredos in the Lady Chapel. Among its decoration are Burton's initials and his rebus of a burr or bush growing from a tun or barrel, as well as the arms of the Berkeley and Clare families. Like much of the rest of the medieval interior of the church, the Lady Chapel was decorated with bright colours, complementing the stained glass windows. Traces of paint survived in the Lady Chapel, and in 1935 the reredos and sedilia were re-painted in their original colours.

For the most of the four centuries of the abbey's existence, the historian is hampered by the paucity of documentary evidence. For the final decades, however, several accounts or 'compotus rolls' provide precise details of income and expenditure. Lacking venerated relics that could attract pilgrims and their offerings, St Augustine's was almost completely dependent upon the rents for its properties in Bristol, the income from its rural estates, and the tithes from its appropriated parish churches. Under Abbot Newland all these sources were carefully managed, and they produced an income of about £700 per annum. Successive abbots lived in considerable style with their own separate households, and each year the abbot's expenses consumed more than 20% of the total income. Taxes, legal costs, hospitality and charity accounted for a further 15%; wages for the numerous servants, housekeeping and maintenance took almost 30%; and candles, books, vestments and the costs of maintaining the regular round of daily services required another 10%. Further expenditure was necessary for the choir school and the grammar school which were maintained within the abbey. All these costs were regarded as essential features of a great monastic house, and left only a small margin for building work or any unusual expenses. It is a tribute to Abbot Newland's careful management that he was able to finance so much building work out of surplus income and without incurring debts.

The 'compotus rolls' throw some light on daily life within the abbey. They reveal the important task of managing the abbey's widespread estates, the supplies of produce brought up the Avon to the abbey, and the sale of surplus corn, malt and bread. The charges for the schoolmaster and the school remind us of the boys who must have provided a lively element within the abbey precinct. It was no doubt the boys from the abbey school who were responsible for the inscribed slate with part of the alphabet on one side and a figure, possibly representing the schoolmaster, roughly drawn on the other, which was found during an excavation in 1992. Expenses for the canons' clothing, food, ale, wine and wages for the numerous abbey servants, together with the costs of the guest house and infirmary, show another aspect of monastic life. The expenditure on vestments, books, candles and the ornaments of the church are a reminder of the regular round of daily services which were the central purpose of the whole institution.

The Berkeley influence and benevolence continued until the end, and in 1521 Maurice, Lord Berkeley, left 'a great portion of money towards the building of the body (nave) of the church of the monastery of St Augustine'. But by this time pressures for reform in the church were growing, and Bristol was strongly affected by the new ideas. Following the 1534 Act of Supremacy, which declared that Henry VIII and not the Pope was supreme head of the Church in England, the process began which was to lead to the suppression of all the religious houses in England. In Bristol the required assent to the Act was signed by Abbot William Burton and eighteen canons. The commissioner sent by Thomas Cromwell in 1535 to enquire into the affairs of the monasteries found nothing wrong at Bristol, even though this commissioner, Richard Layton, was eager to find scandal wherever he could. It was only after the Dissolution that a case before the Ecclesiastical Court revealed that one canon, John Rastle, had been a notorious gambler, and had enticed men to his chamber at the abbey to play at cards with him. No other irregularities have come to light. Although many monastic houses surrendered to the Crown and were suppressed during the years 1536-38, St Augustine's continued. Indeed, even as late as the summer of 1539, when Abbot Burton died, a licence was granted for the election of a successor. Morgan Gwilliam, who had been prior, was chosen, but he survived as abbot for only a few months. On 9 December 1539 the abbot and eleven canons surrendered the monastery to the King's Commissioners and were awarded pensions. Thus four centuries of monastic life came to an abrupt end.

The abbot, Morgan Gwilliam, received a generous pension of £80 per annum. The former canons were granted pensions ranging from £6 to £10 per annum depending on their seniority. Many of the canons later became parish priests or served as chantry priests in Bristol and the surrounding region. There were also 46 officers of the household and servants employed in the abbey, all of whom were paid their wages and dismissed by the Royal Commissioners.

During the course of the suppression or soon afterwards, the old nave of the abbey church and the partly-built walls of the new nave were demolished. When, in 1542 a new cathedral was established using the former monastic buildings, the cathedral church consisted of only the chancel, transepts and central tower.

At the Dissolution the treasures with which the abbey church was furnished passed to the Crown and were dispersed. There can, however, be no doubt of their splendour and value. The beautifully illuminated missal of *c.*1450 has already been mentioned. Its fine workmanship and calligraphy give an indication of the quality of the items that have been lost. The Royal Commissioners in December 1539 also noted many other valuables. These included 526oz of silver plate, 'ornamentes, goodes and catalles (chattels)' worth £103, 'Myteres Garnished with Silver gilte, ragged peerles and counterfette stones', and elaborately embroidered vestments decorated with silver and pearls. These treasures were to be lost forever when the Augustinian canons were expelled from their house.

2   The Cathedral established 1542-1800

The dissolution of the monasteries added considerably to the financial resources of the crown but left it with a large number of redundant buildings. Some were sold off with the monastic estates, constituting a powerful incentive to support the Henrician reformation on the part of the new owners. A number remained. An enterprising council like that of Bristol acquired the chapel to Gaunt's Hospital and thus became the owner of its own chapel — the only local authority to do so. Some became new parish churches, as at Bolton Abbey in Yorkshire, but there were a large number left unused. The English Church had not undergone any major organisational reform since the time of Lanfranc (Archbishop of Canterbury 1070-1090) apart from the establishment of the Dioceses of Ely in 1109 and Carlisle in 1133, during the reign of Henry I. During the period when the various Acts of Parliament were being passed from 1529 onwards, and the monasteries were being dissolved, there had been talk of a major reform of the dioceses. Henry VIII himself had noted down possible new sees. Had this plan been implemented, the Church would have broken free from the diocesan areas, which were still predominantly those of the Anglo-Saxon tribes. There could have been a diocese for each of the English counties. However, it came to nothing. Instead a modest proposal came forward. Bishoprics would be established for new dioceses at Gloucester, Peterborough, Oxford, Chester and Westminster. In neither scheme was Bristol mentioned; but suddenly it was in the plan. Ten months after Gloucester had been set up, the new Diocese of Bristol was established. The city and county of Bristol were taken from Gloucester, three parishes were taken from Bath and Wells, and the Archdeaconry of Dorset was added to it, being taken in its turn from the Diocese of Salisbury. It was an absurd arrangement: 221 out of 256 churches were about 50 miles or more from the episcopal seat. No coherent argument for it can be found, since there are no surviving documents to indicate either what led to the establishment of the diocese or the definition of its area. All that can be said is that there were areas of peculiar jurisdiction and units separated from the mother diocese still in existence at this time, (for example, Croydon is still part of the Diocese of Canterbury) since a single diocesan unit may not have been central to government thinking. Dioceses operated in a much more devolved way at that time, in comparison with the modern style.

It is said that Henry had made some kind of verbal promise about giving Bristol a bishopric, but this is unsubstantiated oral tradition. However, there was a very good argument for establishing a new see in Bristol. It was one of the principal cities of the kingdom; the population of the area was relatively numerous; and it had been the scene of clashes between the reformers and the conservatives. The city had then started to show signs of embracing reformed ideas with some enthusiasm. A royal nominee as bishop was a good way of observing and controlling such an important centre. In this sense an episcopal agent was more important than a cathedral and a chapter, while members appointed directly by the Lord Chancellor would be useful as a way of keeping the citizens in line with the changes and chances of government policy. Dorset could be managed by an archdeacon and overall it produced a diocese not dissimilar in size from the others being set up at about the same time, apart from its geography.

The buildings were in need of repair, as the Crown recognised, while the new Cathedral remained, like the old Abbey, without a nave. Furthermore the Reformers had no particular love of cathedrals. Men like Cranmer were more interested in the use that could be made of the premises for educational purposes than they were in a continual round of worship. It was Stephen Gardiner, representing a more conservative tradition, who stood for cathedrals as places of excellence in music and liturgy. His outlook was to prevail, almost against the odds.

Cranmer's Statutes, promulgated on July 5 1542, described a pattern of cathedral life that had but a short span. By the time Archbishop Laud carried out his visitation in 1634 it had passed away. The establishment was to consist of a dean, six canons residentiary, six minor canons (to include the sacrist, deacon and sub-deacon), six lay clerks, one master of the choristers, six choristers, two masters for the school, four poor people to be maintained by the Cathedral, an under sacrist, a doorkeeper, butler, cook and auditor. Their rates of pay were all specified, from £27 for the dean to 15s for each chorister. Cranmer laid down that there should be a common table for meals, and the provision of cloth and money for livery. The system of emoluments was complicated: various rates were set out for each person attending services, as were the penalties for absence. The precentor had the onerous task of keeping a register and arranging the settlement of accounts. However, the Statutes also stated the number of days on which a person could be absent: 100 days for the dean, 80 for the canons. No mention is made of the pattern of services. The custom of cathedrals should be observed so that there was a constant stream of joy and praise. Most Sundays, too, there was to be a sermon. In many ways the precentor was a pivotal figure, not only in checking attendances but also in ensuring the adequate performance of worship. Hence his job specification states that he was to be older than the rest and eminent for his learning, directing the singing men to make sure that there was no discord in the chanting.

From the Statutes it seems clear that the Crown intended the cathedrals to be religious communities of secular, as opposed to regular, clergy. The Augustinian canons were important in this respect inasmuch as they were all in priests' orders, whereas the monks in other places and orders might not be in holy orders at all. The cathedral life of the 1540s was therefore not dissimilar from the abbey life of the 1530s; even the numbers were approximately the same. In no sense was Bristol to be a parish church, nor was it envisaged that it should justify its existence by some form of utility. It was there so that 'constant prayers and unceasing supplications may be offered decently and in good order' so that 'every day the praise of God may be celebrated with song and rejoicing. We have decreed that God shall be worshipped in this our church with hymns and psalms and continual prayers'. These included 'obsequies to be made for our soul' when Henry should die; and that 'the day of our death be written in the statute-books, upon which same day anniversary obsequies and masses shall for ever be celebrated for us'. Like so much else, this came to be set aside in future years.

Liturgical changes accompanied by major theological shifts soon followed on, all of which affected the style and content of worship in the Cathedral; yet the Statutes themselves were never altered. The 1549 Prayer Book brought services in English, and the monastic hours disappeared, to be replaced by morning and evening prayer. The Mass of the Sarum rite gave way to the Eucharist of 1549 which was little different but was followed soon after by 1552's radical revision, to which there were slight alterations in 1559 and a fundamental re-drafting in 1662. More significantly, daily and even weekly Eucharists disappeared from the life of the cathedrals and parish churches. Within 50 years there might not be more than four a year, though in some places there was a monthly celebration. It is not clear what the practice in Bristol was, but from the attempts made in the seventeenth century there do not seem to have been frequent celebrations. Perhaps the use of copes had ceased; chasubles had certainly disappeared. It was a simpler, plainer liturgical world in which the ministry of the word triumphed over the ministry of the sacrament.

The liturgical changes which followed during the reigns of Edward VI (1547-53) and Elizabeth I (1558-1603) necessitated major changes to the internal arrangements of the cathedral, which we must assume, but cannot prove. The movement away from frequent eucharists and a change in the theology of that sacrament brought about the removal of stone altars and their replacement by wooden tables, which might be brought forward into the choir when required, so that those who truly and earnestly did repent could draw near in faith round it. So the reredos was removed in 1561. The rood, remaining images and other 'ornaments of popish worship' were also ordered to be removed by the government commission appointed for the purpose.

By the early decades of the seventeenth century there had been a reaction to this emphasis upon stark simplicity. Between 1622 and 1632, payments are recorded in the chapter records for the making of statues of the four Evangelists. John Clarke was commissioned to do this work. He was also to make the arch over the choir door and make new stone 'stayers up to the organ and also repair the arches for the twelve prophates before the choir door'. A watercolour of 1830 shows them still in place. They disappeared in the restoration work of the 1860s.

Of the music used we have little knowledge. The older music seems to have been discarded. A *Temporale* of 1360-80, with music for the mass, was taken out of use in 1557 and used, in part, as wrapping material. Some of it survived to be rediscovered and used for the Friends' Festival in 1949.

There were different versions of the Bible available. Some attached great loyalty to themselves, so that when the so-called Authorised Version was produced in 1611 it met with some resistance. The Puritans continued to think that there were more modern versions that the people could more easily understand. Certainly there were words and phrases retained in that translation which had long passed out of common usage. The translators set out to deliberately use archaic language, even though it might be beautiful.

John Selden deeply regretted that a translation had been produced that was so difficult for ordinary people to understand.

Thus Bristol Cathedral and the diocese itself carried through their reformation. Once these changes were made, accepted and established, the life of the Cathedral settled down to a routine that remained unaltered until the middle of the nineteenth century, apart from the suppression of both cathedral and diocese during the Commonwealth.

Seventeenth century England suffered from acute political and religious conflicts, with Bristol at their heart. Interspersed with them were more local disputes. These seem to have centred mainly around relations between the Cathedral and bishop with the mayor and corporation. They were also partly concerned with accommodation and partly with status. The mayor and corporation at this time were expected to attend divine service in the Cathedral; indeed the service might not begin until they arrived, nor continue after they left. In 1577 the government ordered that they should attend, not stand upon ceremony and wait to be fetched in procession by the dean and chapter, preceded by a cross.

In October 1606 the common council ordered that seating should be erected in the Cathedral where the mayor, aldermen, councillors and their wives might sit to hear sermons on Sundays and festival days. At this time there was little seating and small space for a congregation. After some hesitation the Chapter agreed to the proposal and further consented to the removal of the pulpit to a place that fronted the intended seats. The accommodation was described, at the time, as consisting of a gallery, with ornamentation and standing upon pillars, with the centre part reserved for the King or any noble visitors who happened to be present. Underneath were seats for the wives. Chapter took matters a stage further by stipulating that it and the bishop should also find places in the gallery by the side of the mayor. The bishop, John Thornborough, was also Dean of York, and was absent when all this was arranged. When he did arrive in Bristol he was displeased with the new provision, about which he had not been consulted. He wrote to the Archbishop of Canterbury, Richard Bancroft, to complain that it made the Cathedral look like a playhouse. Bancroft was not likely to accept anything that appeared to either diminish ecclesiastical status or enhance lay pretensions. He sent down an order commanding the removal of the gallery. The council was now incensed: it asked for a stay of execution until an appeal had been made both to the Archbishop and to Salisbury, King James's principal minister. Sweeteners were applied in the form of generous travelling expenses. Thornborough ignored the council and the gallery was removed, but at the cost of poor church and state relations in the city. The council forsook the Cathedral, with the consent of the Archbishop, and betook themselves to St Mary Redcliffe. There the matter rested for the time being. It has been argued that a modest replacement gallery was erected, but the council records do not confirm that. Certainly in 1613 there was a resolution to proceed with a replacement but it came to nothing; mainly, it would seem, because of a failure to agree about the allocation of costs.

Dr Robert Wright became bishop of Bristol in March 1623, and immediately set about improving relations with the Corporation. He proposed that the civic seats should be reinstated. A committee was appointed to confer with him, whilst a butt of sack and two hogsheads of claret were sent to him as a token of the city's regard. Later he was made a

*15 Minster House.
H. O'Neill, 1821*

*16 Part of a plan of
Bristol 1568,
William Smith*

Freeman. The seats were leased in perpetuity, and at a cost of £45 were installed on both sides of the choir, the members of the Council being on one side and their wives on the other. At a cost of 15s a gilt branch was also installed for holding the state sword, something which was to cause trouble later.

The Cathedral's arms were changed in 1624 from a representation of the Trinity to which the Church was dedicated, where the Father, Crucified Son and Dove appeared on the obverse with the figure of Henry VIII on the reverse. The new seal had three crowns 'in pale, a saltier cross charged with three fleur de lis and a portcullis'.

When Archbishop Laud became Primate in 1633 he started upon a general visitation. Bristol came under his review in 1634 and, though nothing came of his work, his papers show something of life in the Cathedral during the time of Charles I. There had been changes from the original vision, even though the Statutes had never been altered. Periods of residence were a matter of concern, as they were to be on a number of occasions in the future. Part of the trouble lay in the fact that the dean and the prebendaries were pluralists, something which was a fact for a great many cathedral dignitaries, bishops and incumbents. At Bristol it seems as though the practice had been for one month's residence in the year to be observed; this was regarded as sufficient.

In order to improve Chapter stipends a number of other unspecified appointments had been suppressed. Minor canons were paid a small amount, though this was offset by allowing them to hold other appointments. The salary of the gospeller went to the organist and lay clerks to improve their stipends. A number of them were organists or parish clerks in other churches in the city; the litany was but rarely sung in the Cathedral, probably because of their absence elsewhere. The almsmen were non-resident but gave something to the sexton for the performance of the duties which fell upon them, like sweeping the church and ringing the bells. The common table had disappeared, but the posts of caterer, butler and cook survived for the sake of stipends and patronage. The school master was also the bishop's chaplain, which might not be an onerous appointment since the Bishop was but little in Bristol. However, he was so aged as to be unable to either instruct or supervise the boys. The post of usher had been abolished. The houses of the prebendaries were leased out. The library had been converted to a private house. The common hall for the choir was also rented out, as were several other unnamed properties. The school house had been turned into a tennis court. The Cathedral was used as a through way to the Bishop's Palace and to other houses situated near the cloisters. College Green was in a poor condition, not least because it had been ploughed up by sledges dragging loads of laundered clothes to Brandon Hill where they were left to dry. The Corporation had also erected a whipping post on the Green, whilst people played stop-ball and other games there all day and every day.

The chapter also reported that it was the practice of the Cathedral to conclude the service straightaway, even if matins were not finished, immediately upon the arrival of the mayor and corporation for the sermon. On the other hand, if the service finished and the civic party had not yet arrived, everyone sat in silence until they did so. Thereafter the preacher mounted the pulpit.

Laud sent down a few instructions that resulted in £20 being set aside for repairs, and the same sum for an increase to the stipends of the choristers. The sinecure appointments of those who were to serve the now defunct common table were abolished. The order came in February 1638. By the middle of 1639 Laud and the King were embroiled in the major conflict with the Scots, which was to lead into the Civil Wars and times which would prevent the implementation of Laud's plans.

There was a strong religious element in the Civil Wars. The victorious Parliamentarians held, on the whole, radical views, in which neither bishops nor cathedrals played a part. The places they controlled found both episcopal clergy and their buildings roughly treated. In 1647, episcopacy, cathedrals, deans and canons were all abolished. Their revenues were to be used for the maintenance and enhancement of the ministry elsewhere. Thus the gatehouse of the Cathedral was sold off for £18 3s 4d to John Birch. The Bishop's house and grounds went for £240 to Thomas and John Clark in 1649: they may not have been in good condition.

Although Bishop Thomas Westfield had suffered the loss of his income after the Parliamentarians took the city, he managed to get it restored — even though he was a bishop he was regarded as a person of unexceptionable character, great learning and merit. He died in 1644 without suffering damage to his residence. His successor Thomas Howell was not so fortunate. He was enthroned on April 12 1645, just two months before the Battle of Naseby virtually extinguished Royalist hopes. A short while afterwards Fairfax stormed Bristol. Though his terms of surrender to Prince Rupert showed his humanity, the conduct of others did not. Even though Mrs Howell was lying in labour, the lead was stripped from the roof above her head. She died of exposure, and the Bishop and his children became refugees. The palace became a mill and a malt house. The plan to erect a furnace on the site of the principal altar never came to pass.

The Restoration of the monarchy in 1660 led to the re-establishment of bishops, cathedrals, deans and canons. It also led to the repair and beautification of churches, many of which, especially cathedrals, had suffered during the time of the Republic. The altar that appears in later prints and pictures must date from this post-Restoration period. It was described as gilded, with costly painting, as well as having black and white marble steps. On either side of it were two painted galleries. From the pavement to the base of the east window there were three arches separated by buttresses with crockets and finials. In the centre was an altarpiece of four Corinthian columns enclosing an arch on which was painted a nimbus by Van Somers (1576-1621), which supported an entablature and a circular divided pediment. Regrettably, the descriptions available to us do not give an accurate picture of the altarpiece. However, we are fortunate in having a sketch, albeit unfinished, drawn by A. Montagne. This gives a much better idea of the ornament. It is said to be based on a foreign baroque sarcophagus. On the back of the sketch is written: 'The minster church of Bristol. Proposed altarpiece from designs projected by Mr Inigo Jones'. He lived between 1573 and 1652, but is not known to have undertaken work of this kind, although it could be argued that the altarpiece has features in common with the south porch of St Mary's, Oxford, which is often attributed to him. Perhaps some of Jones's material in the form of designs was used, but the execution could not have been in his lifetime: it would hardly have survived the iconoclasm of the Republic. This altarpiece was removed when the east end was restored in 1839.

The Glemham windows were installed in this post-Restoration period. A new organ

*17 The classical
    reredos*

*18 Medieval screen with
    the organ on it*

was also acquired, and conflict with the corporation was renewed. Bishop Guy Carleton had a colourful past. He had been a belligerent during the Civil Wars and may have had that sort of temperament. He was also the local instrument of the Government as the reaction set in against dissident non-conformists. Given the ecclesiastical temperament of Bristol, tensions could not be far away. The chapter as a whole probably shared the same outlook. Up to 1677 it was the custom of the Cathedral to pray for the corporation before the Church, when the bidding prayer was used. The Bishop ordered this to be altered. Some of the chapter refused compliance and were rebuked for disobedience. Prebendary Crossman (the hymn writer) was threatened with suspension, but it seems clear that the chapter was seeking to improve relations with the Corporation. The councillors responded to episcopal direction by a countermove of their own. The council asserted its right to have the state sword carried erect into the choir before the mayor and corporation as they processed. They further declared that the sword should remain erect throughout the service when chapter insisted that it should be lowered. For a time the councillors remained, with their sword, west of the choir and attended only for the sermon. The next bishop, William Gouston, tried to find a way forward. In the end it was decided that the sword should be carried erect into the Cathedral and then be placed on a cushion.

Although he had become a fervent Roman Catholic, James II declared that he wished toleration for all. He was not believed. Rather it was thought that he wished to promote Roman Catholics to a far more prominent place in public life. The considerable rise in the number of Roman Catholic army officers was taken as being ominous. At the same time James seems to have imagined that the Anglican laity and hierarchy would support his plans, not least because of their standing on the principles of non-resistance and passive obedience. He was mistaken. When he ordered a Declaration of Indulgence to be read out in all Anglican churches he was met with a virtual blank refusal.

James's response to the appeal and petition of the seven bishops, one of whom was the bishop of Bristol, was to put them on trial for seditious libel. They were acquitted. It was now clear to many prominent men that some outside assistance was required. They invited the Prince of Orange, James's nephew and son-in-law, to come over to help. James fled. William, Prince of Orange, and Mary, his wife and James's daughter, became joint sovereigns. Now there was a crisis of conscience and an oath of loyalty was required. Many accepted the *de facto* position and swore; a number did not. They believed that as they had sworn fealty to James they could not swear to another, since James was still alive and had not formally abdicated. In this way episcopalianism was marginalised in Scotland and non-jurors came to notice in England, led by the Archbishop of Canterbury. Amongst those who refused to swear was Canon William Hunt, of the first stall. John Fielding, the Dean, Canons John Rainstorp, Thomas Horne, John Chetwynd, Stephen Crespion and Richard Towgood all subscribed, together with Henry Jones the Chancellor and Bishop Gilbert Ironside, the new Bishop; his predecessor Jonathan Trelawny having been translated to Exeter as a reward, perhaps, for loyalty to the new regime.

The Church of England in the eighteenth century has sometimes been judged unsympathetically. This was partly because it was the basis from which the Utilitarians criticised the Church, and partly because it constituted a good deal of which the Tractarians disapproved. Given the outlook of later times there were deficiencies. In its own time the eighteenth century Church seemed thoroughly integrated into the social structure. However, Bristol features in the description of this deficient Church because of the writings of Thomas Newton, Bishop of Bristol, who held the see for a little over 20 years (1761-82). His main criticism concerned residences maintained by the chapter. Having given the stipends of the chapter as £500 for the dean and about £250 for each prebend, he continued to assert that the usual practice was for the dean to be in residence for three months and the prebends for a month and a half. However, he continued, he had resided in Bristol 'for months together without seeing the face of Dean, Prebendary or anything better than a Minor Canon'. The precentor, then a minor canon, together with the sexton, managed all. This he thought not good enough for the second city of the kingdom, to which many people resorted in order to enjoy the wells. (This was the time when there were high hopes that Hotwells would develop as a spa to rival Bath. Unfortunately the temperature of the water is only 19°C, whereas Bath's is 37°C. The growth never took place. But the Cathedral funerary monuments bear witness to the hopes of some who turned to it for their health and were disappointed.) When these visitors worshipped at the Cathedral they were disappointed to find the dean and the prebends absent. This sad state of affairs, the Bishop believed, was well known in the country. All this gave ammunition to those who were opposed to cathedrals and who would, if they could, abolish deans and canons.

There was justification for such criticisms, but they applied to the Church as a whole and not merely to Bristol. As Laud's visitation papers showed, residence had often come down to almost token proportions. The prebendary stipend was often associated with a stipend derived from elsewhere. They were a 'top-up' in order to produce what was thought to be an adequate competence. A coherent salary system had not yet been developed anywhere in the forces, the Church or politics. Fees, perquisites, and multiple rôles were combined in an *ad hoc* manner to produce a standard of living. We need not assume that the absent prebend was a drone. He had, very likely, an appointment elsewhere, perhaps a benefice where he lived for most of the time and where he exercised his ministry. He came to his cathedral as did the priests of the Temple in Jerusalem when the residence rota required them. Even after the reforms of the nineteenth century the same kind of additional rôles continued to operate. Canons Ainger and Barnett both held major appointments in London and came down to Bristol merely for their residences and necessary chapter meetings. The practice was common.

Bishop Newton did not seem to recognise that he was part of the problem to which he drew attention. The bishopric of Bristol was not well endowed; most of the men appointed hoped for something better later on. Joseph Butler was candid about the meagreness of the stipend and the impossibility of keeping up the state expected of a Spiritual Baron without some extra appointment. Both Butler and Newton held the Deanery of St Paul's, London, which gave them extra resources. Other bishops like Smalridge, Conybeare and Bagor held the Deanery of Christ Church, Oxford. A worshipper at either place might have attended there for some long time before he saw the Dean. Further, it must be remembered that bishops were expected to attend the Parliamentary session as members of the House of Lords. In effect this kept them in London between October and June. When they were free to go down to their dioceses, the Bishop of Bristol had to decide which part should receive his ministrations. His palace was in Bristol, but most of his clergy and their parishes were in Dorset. It would seem as though that archdeaconry did well to see its Bishop every other year. Overall, it is not surprising that wits averred that the Bishop of Bristol never died, he only got translated. The rate of turnover was high compared with the neighbouring diocese of Gloucester, which, though established at about the same time, was better endowed. Newton, despite his solicitations, was never translated. Others like Secker and Butler went to more rewarding appointments. If ever there should be a change in the ecclesiastical climate, the cathedrals as a whole, and not just Bristol, were open to the cold blasts of critical reform.

Whatever else, the Cathedral was well maintained. The words of Browne Willis have sometimes been taken to mean that the building was ill looked after. He wrote that the Cathedral was 'one of the meanest in the Kingdom'. That seems to have been sufficient to rather disregard it. Willis's further comments give the right interpretation. He continued, 'by the generosity and zeal of the present members it is so well-adorned that it wants no cost or art to render it beautiful, and is daily improving and may be said to be kept in good Repair as any church whatsoever. The whole structure is kept so decent that the Example of this Chapter is worthy to be recommended to the imitatyion of our richester and most ancient Cathedral.'

This comment, however, does not give a description of the buildings during this period. For this we have to turn to the work of William Barrett in a work published in 1789. The plan shows the layout as it was in 1788. He gives the length of the building as 175ft and the breadth as 128ft. The choir is said to be 100ft long and the tower 127ft high. The key to the letters is:

A   The main entrance from College Green
B   The entrance to the Elder Lady Chapel
C   The entrance to the cloisters
D   The Sub Sacrist's vestry
E   Font and entrance to the Consistory and Registry
F   Stone pulpit and seats for the Bishop, Dean, Prebendaries and Corporation
G   Choir stalls: seventeen either side
H   Bishop's throne and stall for the Archdeacon of Dorset
    N.B. Not shown by letter on the plan
I   Vestry, Sealing House, St Mary's chapel
J
K   High altar and steps
L   Chapter house
M Tombs of the Lords Berkeley
N   Tombs of the Newtons
O   Tombs of the Canonical Abbots
P   Tomb of Bishop Bush
Q Tomb of Sir John and Lady Young
R
S   Codrington monument

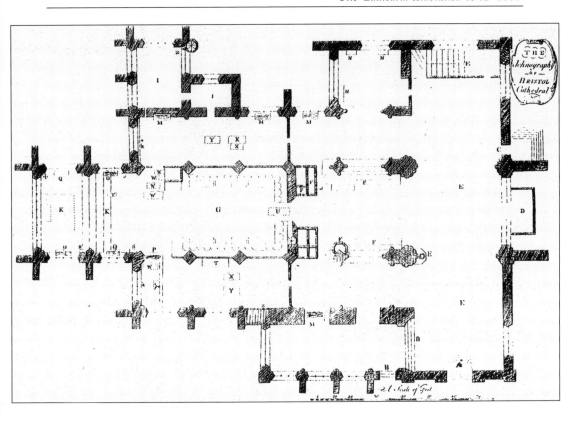

19 Barrett's plan of cathedral in 1780s

T Tomb of Sir Charles Vaughan
U Founder's grave; new site of monument
V
W Gravestones of Bishops Howell, Westfield and Ironside
X Gravestones of Deans Tonsons, Crossman and Towgood
Y Gravestones of Prebendaries
Z Staircase
+ Monument to Mrs Weekes.

We can see from this plan where some of the monuments were situated originally, before the renovations of the nineteenth century. The sub sacrist's vestry against the interior west wall is to be noticed, together with the use of the St Mary Chapel (now the Berkeley Chapel) as a work place. The most significant change from later times is the statement that there were 34 stalls in the choir, 17 on either side. Now there are 28, with 14 on either side. Six have disappeared in the nineteenth century, and with them, no doubt, six misericords, as to whose design and theme we can have no knowledge.

Barrett then describes the rest of the site. The chapter house is stated as being to the south of the church and to be 56 steps by 18, since he uses the measurements given by

William of Worcester, taken by him about 1480. Entrance to the chapter house, Barrett states, is through the east cloister which stands complete. It is also the way to the Bishop's palace, with its garden and walks that were brought into existence because the Bishop negotiated land leases by Trinity Street (now Steps) which gave him more space. To the south of the east cloister he refers to the Fraterhouse (Refectory), which he says Worcester measured as 26 by 16 steps. The south cloister and the west cloister have been removed, writes Barrett, but the north cloister remains. It had a stone-covered sloping roof. This could have served no useful purpose, but merely stood on its own at the bottom of the gardens of the houses which were built on the site between the west wall and the gatehouse. The cloisters measured 103ft every way.

West of the area between the private houses and the Deanery stood the gatehouse, which he describes as being very fine, well preserved and little damaged by time. To the west of the gatehouse was the Deanery. This, he writes, appears to be a good house, which was repaired by Dean Creswick (1730-39) and rebuilt almost in its entirety by Dean Warburton (1757-60). We have no knowledge of the housing of the clergy; there is but one photograph which shows the east end of the Deanery as it abuts the gatehouse. The Bishop's palace, which has now disappeared completely, receives considerable attention. It had fallen into disrepair by the early eighteenth century. Bishop Smalridge (1714-19) repaired it, but it again fell into a poor state. Bishop Butler (1738-50) spent nearly £5000 on a virtual total restoration. The house could now be regarded as very convenient, with many of the rooms being both large and 'ornamented in a grand manner'. The chapel, which was only 15ft by 11ft, was wainscoted in cedar. The arms of some bishops and abbots appear to have been painted upon glass. It was Butler who negotiated some kind of land exchange with the prebendaries that enabled him to give the house some garden and walks. 'The whole house is a handsome and commodious dwelling, which his lordship and the succeeding bishops have made their place of residence for about five months of the year, during which time once a week they keep an open table for all the clergy and gentry'.

These repairs undertaken by Butler could throw light upon two significant features of the abbey. When the repairs were being undertaken, a parcel of plate inadvertently fell to the floor, which was so decayed that it went right through. Examination of the scene revealed a great many human bones, instruments of iron, which Barrett does not specify, together with a passageway which led to where the bones were stored. It has often been supposed that the Bishop's house had earlier been the lodgings of the Abbot. But having regard to the general plan of many monasteries, the location of this building to the south of the church and east of the cloister indicates that it might well have been the infirmary of the abbey, near to which could have been the abbey's charnel house. The 'Gothick' imagination of the later eighteenth century thought that the room must have been a dungeon where criminal canons were left to rot. It was certainly not the town gaol. There is nothing to suggest that the abbey suffered from a procession of criminal disobedient clergy. The location of the Abbot's lodgings must be found elsewhere. The area immediately to the south of the gatehouse is one possibility, since the function of the Minster House which was excavated recently is unclear. The excavation could be held to show that this was where guests were accommodated. If this is so, it would not have been unusual for the Abbot's residence to have been in the same block or nearby.

Finally, Barrett comments on the pleasantness of College Green. Formerly it was the graveyard of the abbey. Now it is laid out in pleasant walks with rows of lime trees, much frequented by 'the gay, the beaux and belles of Bristol to walk in, as the Mall is in London'. There were also fine houses round part of it, particularly alongside Gaunt's Hospital Chapel, and when they were built many skulls and bones were dug up. Unfortunately there is no dating evidence for the age at which these burials took place. In the midst of the Green stood the High Cross. In order to create more space for a street-widening scheme it was removed, after which it deteriorated. Dean Barton (1768-81) ordered it to be given to Stourton (Stourhead), where the Dean's brother was the rector. There it adorned the garden of Mr Hoare.

No mention is made of the Cathedral school, nor is there any description of any of the canons' houses. For that we have to rely upon Canon Sydney Smith — famous for his wit and reforming sentiments. Though he does not actually describe his house, a good deal is implied. It must have been large and spacious, even though he called it 'snug and parsonic'. There was stabling for seven horses and room for four carriages. From his windows facing south he could see the masts of the West Indiamen docked in the harbour. These houses, the episcopal palace and many of the other Cathedral buildings were to be swept away in riots. Many of them were never replaced.

3 The Cathedral restored 1800-1970

Far more than the war which led to the independence of the American colonies was the influence of the French Revolution (1789). The execution of Louis XVI, the fall of the aristocracy and the flight of many of its members to England, together with Napoleon's imperialism stimulated a conservative, even reactionary mood in Britain. Even after the fall of Napoleon this fear of change continued. The new industrial towns of the North and the Midlands were producing a new commercial middle class as well as an industrial proletariat. Both were anxious to become part of the political structure of the country; neither had, as yet, any place in it. These became restless times. There were riots, of which the best known was the Peterloo Rally in Manchester (1819) where not only did the situation get out of hand but which ended up with the charge of the Yeomanry and the use of sabres. Gradually the governments of the day gave way, but not before putting up considerable resistance. In the end the problems of Irish politics forced even the ultra-conservative Tories, led by Wellington, to repeal the Test Act (1828) and to carry through Catholic Emancipation (1829), for which Sydney Smith had argued and preached before the Mayor and Corporation of Bristol. The 1830 Revolution in France, which removed Charles X, stimulated the reform movement afresh in Britain. The Tory government fell, to be replaced by a Whig administration led by Earl Gray (1830). The members were committed to parliamentary reform. A Reform Bill was brought forward. It went forward by a majority of one on the Second Reading, only to be defeated by amendments at the Committee stage. On April 19 1831, Gray secured a dissolution of parliament. A hard-fought and bitter election campaign followed, in which public opinion was warmly for 'The Bill, the whole Bill and nothing but the Bill'. The election result was a Whig triumph. On September 21 1831 the new House of Commons passed a second Reform Bill by a majority of 109, but the House of Lords threw it out. This vote was to inflict irreparable damage upon Bristol Cathedral and Diocese.

The Second Reform Bill was lost on October 8 1831. Parliament was prorogued; a new Bill was to be prepared and there was vigorous campaigning. The failure of the Bill brought serious extra-parliamentary agitation. Two London newspapers appeared in mourning, muffled peals of bells were rung and there were riots in major cities like Nottingham and Derby. Worst of all was Bristol. The city already had a reputation for violence, and shortages prompted riots in the markets. During the early part of the nineteenth century the practice of hiring 'bludgeon men', supposedly to maintain the peace, resulted in fighting. During elections the Steadfast Society (the local Tory club) used to seal off the streets leading to the hustings. Faction fights broke out in the narrow streets; the Guildhall was stoned and the windows of the Mansion House were broken.

20 View of cathedral in 1830s showing surviving house

21 Chapter house in eighteenth century, with window cut into south wall and with fireplace installed

Trouble, therefore, could have been expected. Quite apart from the angry protests at the fall of the Reform Bill, there were those in the city who wanted the reform of the Corporation on account of the way in which it ran the local authority. Violence on the streets was likely to occur, and for a variety of causes which would combine.

On October 24 1831 the Bishop of Bath and Wells, George Henry Law, came to consecrate the church of St Paul at Bedminster, then in his diocese. Though the son of a Whig bishop, he had voted against the Reform Bill. He was met by a hostile crowd who shouted abuse and chanted 'Reform, we will have reform'. As he drove away his carriage was pelted with mud. The press had already denounced the bishops as enemies of the people and a large number of pamphlets were appearing in which the church as a whole, and the clergy in particular, were condemned for their opposition to reform. The votes of the bishops in losing the Second Bill when it went to the Lords were held to be critical. It was their vote, argued the critics, that destroyed it. Whether the voting figures ought to be construed in that way may be doubtful: the statistics were less important than the perception. Ardent campaigners for change thought that it was so.

On the morning of Saturday October 29, the mayor and corporation rode out to Totterdown to meet and then escort their recorder into the city, to which he had come for the gaol delivery, which was in ordinary circumstances a simple, regular and uncontroversial event. The recorder was Sir Charles Wetherell who had been Attorney General in the government of the Duke of Wellington. Wetherell had opposed both the

22 The discarded doctors of the church

First and the Second Reform Bills, and the fact was known in Bristol. Anticipating possible protests, the civic officials had brought forward the time of the meeting to 10am in the hope that trouble could be avoided. They also provided themselves with a force of special constables; these had been hired because insufficient volunteers had come forward from the men of property. But bringing forward the meeting by some five hours achieved nothing. As soon as Wetherell's coach came into view the catcalls, boos and hisses commenced. The procession set off as soon as the recorder had joined the mayor in his coach, surrounded by a badly organised party of special constables and preceded by ceremonial trumpeters, whose fanfares heralded their approach to the unsympathetic crowds which lined the route. The cavalcade was subjected to constant attack; there were shouts and missiles and quite inadequate protection for the official party. Finally the Guildhall was reached — it had taken more than an hour to cover just over a mile. However, little damage had been done, and the crowd was boisterous rather than vicious.

When Wetherell left the Guildhall en route for the Mansion House the situation deteriorated. Stones were thrown and the recorder was injured. Several constables ran into the crowd and made random arrests. The mayor and the other magistrates had urged forbearance on the constables but now the situation became more violent with the charges of the constables. The mayor and the magistrates gave no lead, and the attitude of the crowd turned ugly. At 4pm the rioting started in earnest, undeterred by the nearby

23 North choir aisle 1830s

presence of troops that had not, however, been deployed. The Riot Act was read to no avail; the crowd did not disperse and instead the attack on the Mansion House began in earnest. Wetherell was clearly under threat but escaped disguised as a postillion. Violence continued on into the evening with an attack on the Mansion House where the windows were smashed. The cavalry went into action. First sabres and then pistols were used to clear the streets. The rioters fled. It was 12.30am on Sunday October 30. Quiet was maintained until dawn broke. At 8.30am there were further attacks on the Mansion House, which was thoroughly ransacked and the wine cellar looted. The city now had a large body of drunken rioters. The Mayor escaped to College Green. Round about 2pm rioters moved to the Bridewell where the prisoners taken on the previous day were being held. Armed with hammers and other instruments they got in, and after a fierce fight released the prisoners. Next the New Gaol was attacked successfully and the prisoners were released. After that there was some kind of meeting to decide what should be attacked next. The four toll booths at Prince Street bridge, the Wells and St Philips were selected. At 4.30pm the mob arrived at the Gloucester County Prison at Lawfords Gate. Again all the prisoners were set free and the building was torched. Smaller groups went on to attack a variety of other premises in a random manner. The rioters had the free run of the city. The magistrates did nothing; no one in authority, apparently, could decide what to do.

At about 8pm a large group of rioters decided to attack the Bishop's Palace, as the home of a reactionary, and attacked the Cathedral en route. The arrival of about 20 troopers restrained them for a while, but since the soldiers remained passive and then departed, the rioters applied sledge hammers and crowbars. To shouts of 'The King' and 'No bishops' the Cathedral archives and library were destroyed by the mob. Other buildings were attacked and the chapter house was seriously damaged. The body of the church was only saved by the prompt action of the sub sacrist, William Phillips. He managed to slam the door between the cloister and the south transept, shouting that the Cathedral belonged to the people and no one else. It saved the church and his brave action is commemorated on a plaque near the crucial door. The Bishop's house, however, was totally destroyed. It was never rebuilt and all trace of it has been lost. The Bishop, having preached in the morning, had already fled, being known as an opponent of the Reform Bill. Bishop Robert Gray had refused to cancel this service on account of the riots, though the Mayor had ordered its cancellation on Saturday evening. Now there was no episcopal residence. Gray died in 1834 and his successor Joseph Kay moved on to Ely in the same year. By the time James Henry Monk arrived in 1836 the government of Lord Melbourne had considered what should be done at Bristol, and that was radical indeed.

The Church as a whole was in dire straits. Unpopular for the rôle of the bishops in the reform programme, it was also subjected to a barrage of attacks of which the most telling was the anonymous publication *The Extraordinary Black Book* which appeared in 1831, allegedly giving a true account of Church revenues and their distribution. Written in a spirit hostile towards the Church, it contained enough truth to assist the Third and successful Reform Bill and the reforming ecclesiastical legislation which followed. The sheer cost of the Church was remarked upon; far more than the Church in France which had a much larger population. Wealth was combined with a lack of piety and notorious abuses. The bishops were political nominees — a hit at a quarter of a century of Tory conservative rule — upon whom so many resources were squandered. The clergy in general had no interest in education. They were stimulated by jealousy of Dissent and founded King's College merely as a protest against the University of London, that 'godless institution in Gower Street'. The revenues were extracted from the people in a vexatious way on the basis of a doubtful authority. Church property, it was argued, was held on trust for services rendered to the state. It was public and not private; the state had the right to resume it, should it see fit. While the book recognised that the bulk of the work was done by a large number of clergy who received meagre stipends, with some exception, they compensated for this situation by operating a system of pluralism: one third of them, it was said, had succumbed to this vice and that also included bishops and other senior members of the hierarchy. The law with regard to such a matter was applied laxly, if at all.

The writer had his own programme for reform. The incomes of bishoprics should be equalised; the income of poor benefices should be augmented by money taken from rich ones; episcopal patronage, pluralities and sinecures should be abolished; and tithes should be sold to the landowner or commuted for a land tax. The following year, in 1832, Lord Henley proposed a draft scheme. There should be a permanent body of commissioners in whom all episcopal and cathedral properties should be vested; surplus money should be used to augment poor benefices; pluralities were to be limited, residence enforced, the translation of bishops forbidden, and new sees created whose occupants would not sit in the House of Lords. The levels of stipend were to be fixed; with a few exceptions all bishoprics were to be equal. Some deaneries were to merge with bishoprics. Canons of cathedrals were to be forbidden to hold other preferment except in the cathedral city; bishops were to retire with a pension or be sidelined with the appointment of coadjutors. And finally, the patronage of the Crown was to be vested in a Minister for Ecclesiastical Affairs and ten unpaid commissioners. It was this state of affairs that led Thomas Arnold to say that as it was at present constituted, no power on earth could save the Church. He turned his energies to writing an alternative programme in his *Principles of Church Reform*, in which cathedrals played no significant part.

Salvation did come to the Church through the efforts of Sir Robert Peel and Bishop Blomfield of London. The basis of the programme was the former's Tamworth Manifesto. Together they worked their way through the programme. The first report of the government commission into the state of the Church recommended the establishment of two new sees: Manchester and Ripon; a proposal that was to affect Bristol profoundly. Dorset was to revert to Salisbury, which would leave the diocese of Bristol as no more than the medieval city and county. This truncated diocese was to be joined with Gloucester to produce a joint diocese, with one bishop and two cathedrals. Capitular and episcopal property were dealt with radically. For the latter, equalisation of income was secured at the expense of the richer sees. The occupants of the poorer bishoprics should then receive between £4000 and £5000 a year. Capitular bodies were dealt with in a second report issued on March 4 1836. There were sweeping changes. No attention was given to any particular local circumstance; instead a standard organisation was described. With few exceptions, of which Bristol was not one, each chapter should consist of a dean and four residentiary canons. All other titles were to be abolished. The lands of suppressed stalls, rich prebends and sinecure rectories and other benefices were to be vested in the ecclesiastical commissioners, who should apply the income to the augmentation of poor benefices. The system of fines on the leases of benefices should go, to be replaced by a system of short leases. Much capitular patronage, which had often benefited capitular families, passed into the hands of bishops. It was thought that bishops might have a sharper awareness of the force of public opinion, to say nothing of a greater sense of public duty than could be expected of self-regarding chapters. Evidently it was thought that the bad press which the bishops had received on account of the reform bills would give them a more acute sense of the expectations which the public had of them. In the event some bishops did not rise above temptation. Canon Sydney Smith, who had lately moved from Bristol Cathedral to St Paul's in London, in his *Letter to Archdeacon Singleton* protested against the favour shown to bishops like Bathurst of Norwich who were tinged with nepotism and inclined to neglect their duties.

Lord Melbourne succeeded Peel as Prime Minister in April 1835, and at an early date brought forward three bills that embraced much contained in the report. The various bills were passed during 1836 and 1838, by which time the joint diocese of Bristol and Gloucester was established to make way for the Bishopric of Manchester. The amalgamation of the two Welsh sees of St Asaph and Bangor never did occur, since neither bishop left, but the Diocese of Ripon did come into existence in 1836. Meanwhile, the principle of having 26 bishops in the House of Lords on the basis of a rota of seniority began.

At the end of this period of reform, Bristol had been changed like the other cathedrals, but shared a bishop. The bishop's house was damaged beyond repair, many of the Cathedral buildings, notably the chapter house, were also in a parlous state. The number of canons had been reduced, and the close with its canonical housing had also been destroyed. A programme of recovery was necessary. It took time. During 1846 the chapter almost came to a decision to end choral services, but in the end did not — that was the nadir. Within a decade the English choral tradition was reviving well. Cathedrals became centres of musical excellence, even if in Bristol the salary was low and the clerks formed singing groups which entertained the public. The next significant development was the mid-century restoration.

The Cathedral was transformed during the second half of the nineteenth century, at the end of which it had virtually taken the form in which it exists today. Gilbert Elliott had become dean in 1850. He realised how the population of the city was growing, making better seating provision and more space essential. In addition, the restoration of some stained glass was necessary. A start was made with the stained glass, but more significantly in 1859 the chapter resolved to consult G.G. Scott and J.S. Pope, having decided that it was desirable to create more space for public worship. The Victorian religious revival was on its way. No thought seems to have been given at this time to the enlargement of the truncated Cathedral, and only an interior rearrangement was contemplated. With these terms of reference, Scott submitted a report in which he proposed the opening up of the Cathedral, though in the end he disclaimed all responsibility for what actually happened. More space was created by reducing the choir by one bay at the westernmost end, and the choir screen was removed. This was of course the medieval pulpitum which had been moved from the Carmelite Friars in 1542 (and which must have been earlier than that in its original construction). It was a solid screen with a single entrance, such as have survived at Manchester and York. If there was to be more space for public worship and if the congregation were to be able to see the officiants and choir, then its fate was sealed. A new screen in the Early English style replaced it in 1860, made out of stone and marble.

However good it might have been, the Renatus Harris organ had to be removed to another position and while that might not have been serious, the failure to connect the new screen to anything else left it in limbo. As *The Ecclesiologist* put it, the viewer was reminded of a gate to a field where the hedges had been taken away. The choir stalls were moved eastwards and suffered some damage. It may have been at this time that six choir stalls were lost, together with their misericords. There was some Victorian woodwork put in to repair the damage sustained. The repairs to the sanctuary also occasioned criticism. In the exaggerated style that was sometimes used by nineteenth century critics, a writer averred that the tiles and paving would disgrace a railway station. The plain white, yellow, brown, blue and green tiles were bad enough: for them to be laid out in the pattern of a draughtboard was awful. Further, there were no patterned tiles. Gas lighting was also installed, which might be thought a progressive measure, but this too came under the critic's lash, since the standards were placed on large stone bases of hideous and ridiculous design. Whether the total effect was to be considered aesthetically unsatisfactory we cannot know, because virtually all of this restoration work disappeared in subsequent alterations. However poor the visual result might have been, the primary objective was attained. There was more space for public worship.

The main leadership in restoring and enlarging the Cathedral came into the hands of Canon John Pilkington Norris. The Dean had remarried in 1863 Frances Geils, who was an inveterate traveller. Elliot accompanied her and was therefore absent from the Cathedral for long periods. Norris was appointed as a Residentiary Canon in 1864. Shortly afterwards, in 1865, the Bristol Improvement Committee wished to buy the Deanery for the purpose of creating a new road along the north side of the Cathedral between the area of St Augustine the Less and the Hotwells. At the same time others in the chapter seem to have been considering the erection of shops on the site where the old nave had been. Excavations in this area revealed the foundations of a porch and wall belonging to the new nave that Abbot Newland proposed to build but was never able to accomplish. The discovery acted as a trigger for vision. The newly appointed Canon John Norris did not arrive in time to save the Deanery, but he did rally support for something better. In 1866 the Chapter received a letter written on behalf of many of the citizens of Bristol which declared the imperfect state of the Cathedral as both a reproach to the city and a hindrance to the development of the usefulness of the building. It was Norris who drove the scheme ahead, in every respect, not least in the raising of funds. He even secured a donation from Mr Gladstone. The money was raised speedily and with enthusiasm. While civic pride played its part, Norris was the dynamo, with the Dean and the rest of the chapter quiescent.

This stimulated action. G.E. Street was appointed architect, and on April 17 1868 work began upon the construction of the new nave for which the Abbey and Cathedral had waited so long. Regrettably a house at the West end known variously as the Prior's Lodging or the Minster House was destroyed; though there may have been no alternative if the Cathedral was to be completed. Once the nave was completed work could begin on the towers, which were completed after Street's death in 1888. J.L. Pearson took over from Street. He brought the choir back to the position it occupies in 1999 by moving it three bays westward so that it occupied the same site as its medieval predecessor. Pearson was also responsible for the reredos (1899) and the choir screen (1904).

The restoration programme was completed in 1907 with the modernisation of the Cathedral organ. Though there had been modest alterations both in the later eighteenth and early nineteenth centuries, the instrument remained substantially the Renatus Harris instrument of 1685. In 1860 it was moved from the choir screen on its demolition, to be installed in the north choir aisle. J.W. Walker & Sons transformed the instrument, preserving only the best of the pipe-work and wooden organ fronts which are excellent examples of seventeenth century wood carving. The result was one of the best organs in the English Romantic tradition. While the musical style of the period was moving towards a heavier, even brutal, tone, the Walkers effectively balanced this modern idiom with the restrained old pipe-work, thereby achieving a more balanced effect. It is this that has made the Bristol Cathedral organ so outstanding. By 1989 the organ had needed little repair, but was ageing. A conservative restoration was carried out by N.P. Mander Ltd, with Nicolas Kynaston as the organ consultant. Architecturally the solid panels were replaced by wooden grilles designed by Alan Rome, the Cathedral Architect, and the opportunity was taken to restore a number of wooden urns which had been removed in 1860. They were attached to the north-east corner on wooden brackets.

The clergy who have served at the Cathedral during the course of its history compose an interesting group. We should not expect them to be national figures. They were appointed to serve a local community, but a number of them did reach a wider public. They were not expected to be radical figures. The nature of life in both Church and state tended to preclude that, but within their resources they guarded that which had been delivered to them. In some ways the system of pluralities made that wider contribution possible since it gave them a degree of financial security which was often combined with relatively light ecclesiastical duties. Some of the earlier canons are shadowy figures but are not without significance. The new cathedrals needed to be staffed after they were reconstituted. It was not unusual to find that old monks became new canons. The first dean, William Snow, had been prior at Bradenstoke, the first Bishop Prior at Edington. As late as 1556 Richard Hughes was appointed to the Cathedral where he had previously been one of the pre-Reformation Augustinian canons.

Three canons stand out as figures of literature: one for a hymn and the others for more substantial writing. Samuel Crossman's hymn 'My song is love unknown' is still in general use. Though written in the post-Restoration period it has escaped from the convoluted imagery and style of the Jacobean and early Stuart periods. The language is clear, simple, direct and timeless. Sydney Smith came to Bristol with a national reputation: he had been a founder of the *Edinburgh Review*, and was a well-known campaigner and pamphleteer whose hopes of high office were restrained by his Whiggish ideas in a time of Tory dominance. A window of opportunity occurred in 1828 when the Lord Chancellor determined to appoint him; although he deplored his politics he admired him personally. He came to Bristol where he made his views known in his sermons. Although he read them, his style and content were attractive. People would wait outside the Cathedral for it to open, and then when the doors were opened they would dash for the best seats. Canon Richard Hakluyt wrote of the voyages of the great Elizabethan seamen, who became a national legend, and his chronicles are still in print.

Francis Pigou, the Dean from 1891 to 1916 and thus spanning the period during which the Cathedral restoration was completed and an independent bishopric re-established, is the only Cathedral dignitary to have left anything approaching a personal memoir. He moved to Bristol after having been Dean of Chichester, which in some ways could be considered an odd move. With the expected restoration of a separate diocese, it may have been expected that an experienced senior clergyman would be an advantage in Bristol. When he wrote *Odds and Ends* it was the work of a priest who had considerable experience of cathedral and diocesan life.

Pigou also adds some details of Cathedral arrangements. The church was open daily from 10am until 5pm, with 200 seats in the Eastern Lady Chapel and 100 in the Elder which, he notes, had been used formerly as a store. During his tenure the offertory was introduced, a practice which had been resisted in the Church as a whole, because it was considered improper. With some pride he records that Bristol was the first cathedral to install electricity for lighting and for blowing the organ. He was amused that the system failed during Evensong when the words were being read: 'The light shineth in darkness and the darkness comprehendeth it not'. He also notes that it cost £100 to be married in the cathedral. He ends by writing that to be associated with canons of like mind and common desire was not only a sacred trust but a great privilege.

There were also great characters, of whom Dean Blackburne is one of the best known. His autobiography *From Trooper to Dean* charts a course from a soldier in the ranks of the army during the Second Boer War, through the appointments of the Church via a Canonry at St George's Windsor to the Deanery of Bristol. When the 1939 war broke out it proved to be timely, since Queen Mary, the Queen Mother stayed at nearby Badminton, where the Dean was able to exercise an informal ministry to her. Canon Freeman was incumbent of Burton-on-Trent when at the age of 68 he was appointed a Canon of Bristol, where he became famous for the inside of 20 years for his preaching, informed by wide reading and expressed with a great range of literary allusions. The contribution of Dean Douglas Harrison has yet to be assessed, but it must be highly significant. Not only did he steer the cathedral through the liturgical reforms of the 1960s but he also carried out a major work of restoration, without distorting the heritage of the later nineteenth century work. His work is commemorated in a carved head stone where he looks down, with his favourite pipe between his teeth.

The chapter of later years has undertaken diocesan responsibilities of a substantial kind and offered a home to a variety of related church activities, enabling them to find premises until they were able to launch out on their own. These activities relate more to the life of the diocese than they do to the Cathedral; yet they are important for the Cathedral since they display a chapter sympathetic to the needs of a diocese, prepared to pioneer and support the different kinds of ministry needed at the present time. The priests who made up the Chapter of Bristol Cathedral in the second half of the twentieth century — whatever other weaknesses they may have had they cannot be charged with indifference to the needs of the area, nor with being inward-looking nor of a reactionary spirit. There may now be a change in the wind and these characteristics could be regarded less favourably than they were; but, at any rate, for the perceived needs and situation of the post-war decades they then seemed right and useful. Whether the future will judge them as the Victorians judged the eighteenth century is another matter.

4 Romanesque architecture and sculpture

Above the confines of the prelate's seat
An old cathedral, venerably great,
From rising ground a bulky building rears,
And points of time in rugged aspect bears.
Injurious time! thy keenest rage employ,
And gnaw with envy what you can't destroy;
Whilst inward worship shews a cleanly face,
And true devotion adds a second grace,
Omnipotent Eternity protects the place.

W Goldwin M.A., published 1712 (Fellow of King's, Cambridge, and *Master of Bristol Grammar School)*

A visit to Bristol Cathedral today reveals a building of which the earliest parts appear to date from the middle decades of the twelfth century. These represent the surviving fragments from the Abbey founded by Robert Fitzharding in 1140 and built over the succeeding thirty years. The precise dates and sequence of these Romanesque buildings are not clear and may never be so, but the available evidence has been thoroughly trawled over the last 25 years and it is generally agreed that the east end of the church was ready for use by *c.*1159 and that the building was complete by *c.*1170. Of the fragments which remain, the most intact are the lower storey of the Abbey gatehouse situated to the west of the church and the chapter house to the south of the south transept and situated off the east cloister walk. However, they may not represent the earliest medieval masterpieces from the Abbey. More enigmatic, though equally famous, is the sculpted stone panel, 1.7m in height, which is now displayed in the south transept. Any investigation of the early remains of St Augustine's Abbey must begin with this monumental carving of the Harrowing of Hell.

The Harrowing of Hell panel

Soon after the Bristol Riots of 1831, major repairs were carried out in the chapter house. It was then decided to lower the floor — it had been raised 3ft in 1713 — and during the consequent digging about a dozen medieval coffin lids were found. In amongst these was

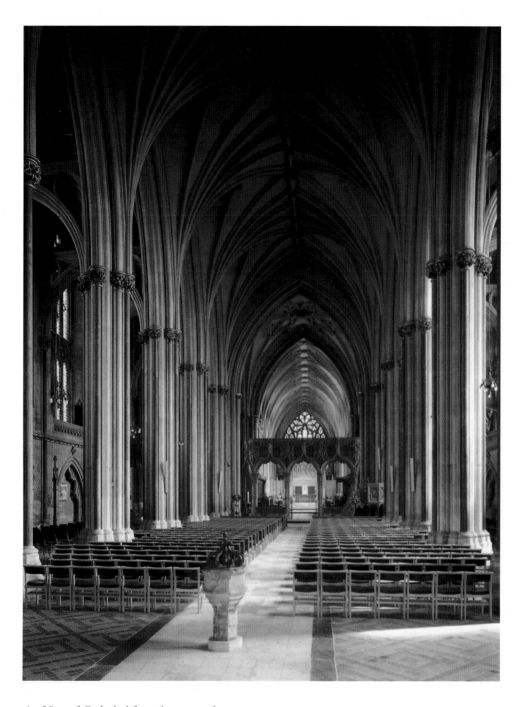

1   *View of Cathedral from the west end*

2   *Glemham window and Codrington Monument*

3   Chapter house

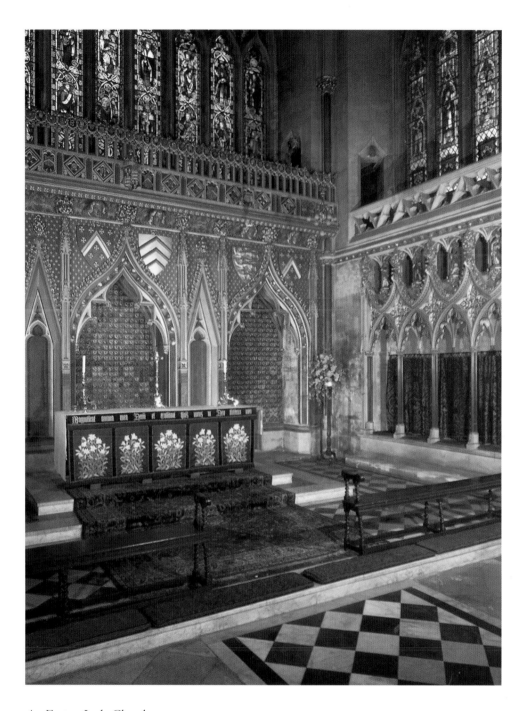

4   *Eastern Lady Chapel*

5   *View of the cathedral from the south west*

6   *Eastern Lady Chapel detail*

7   *The New window*

8   *The Harrowing of Hell stone*

9 Capital heads

10 Roof bosses

11 Middleton monument

THE MEMORY OF JOHN MIDDLETON, ESQUIRE, OF CLIFTON,
WHO DEPARTED THIS LIFE APRIL 5TH 1866, AGED 96 YEARS.

12 Bishop Bush tomb

13 Tomb of abbot

Sacred
To the Memory
Of
M.ʳˢ Eliz.ᵀᴴ Draper
In whom
Genius & Benevolence
Were united.

She died Auguſt 3.ᵈ 1778, aged 35.

14 Draper Memorial

15 *Portrait of Eliza Draper*

16 Tomb of Abbot David

17 Memorial to Dean Pigou

18 Powell Memorial

Bristol! to worth & genius ever just,
To thee our POWELL'S dear remains we trust
Soft as the Stream thy sacred Springs impart,
The milk of human kindness warm'd his heart;
That heart wch every tender feeling knew,
The soil where pity, love, & friendship grew,
Oh let a faithfull friend with grief sincere
Inscribe his tomb, & drop the heartfelt tear,
Here rest his praise, here found his noblest fame!
All else a bubble or an empty name.

G. COLMAN

In the Year 1811
This Monument was repaired and beautified by the direction of ANN MARTINDALE
Youngest Daughter of the deceased WILLIAM POWELL,
from the great duty respect and veneration in which she holds the Memory of
her departed Father.

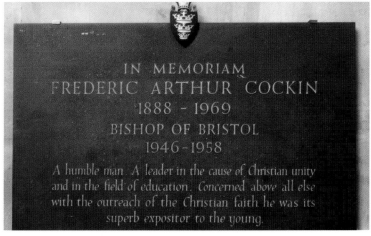

IN MEMORIAM
FREDERIC ARTHUR COCKIN
1888 - 1969
BISHOP OF BRISTOL
1946-1958

A humble man. A leader in the cause of Christian unity
and in the field of education. Concerned above all else
with the outreach of the Christian faith he was its
superb expositor to the young.

19 Memorial to
Bishop Cockin

20 Jesse window

21 Choir stalls detail

23 Martyrdom of St Edmund

24 *War Memorial window*

25 *Choir stall detail*

the carved panel of the Harrowing of Hell. When the panel was found it too had been serving as a coffin lid, although by no means all scholars agree with that as its original purpose. Certainly it is rather broad in relation to its height for such a function: the top is slightly narrower than the bottom and the subject matter is very elaborate in comparison with other surviving English funerary slabs of the early medieval period. Moreover, there is the possibility that although found in the company of coffin lids, the slab was never used for such a purpose. When the floor was raised in 1713 infill would have been needed. No doubt on such a site old coffin lids would have been available to fulfil the requirement. Perhaps, too, this piece of carving was lying redundant and the builders of Queen Anne's reign, not renowned for their sympathy for their early medieval heritage, may well have consigned the barbarous slab to lie alongside the coffin lids. At a later date in the eighteenth century, for example, the architect James Wyatt showed scant interest for many of the medieval furnishings of Salisbury Cathedral when he supervised major restoration work there. If the carving had been lying beneath the twelfth century chapter house floor, why was it only found in the nineteenth century when the raised eighteenth century flooring was removed and taken back almost to its original twelfth century level? This strongly implies that the coffins lay above the level of the twelfth century floor and not below it. If the panel only joined the company of medieval coffins in the eighteenth century, the possibility of its original use in a funerary context becomes yet more tenuous. If not a funerary panel, however, what then was the original context of the stone? Many ideas have been proposed, but before considering these it is necessary to describe the sculpture and its iconography.

As a narrative, the story of Christ's Harrowing of Hell derives from a fifth or sixth century apocryphal account known as the Gospel of Nicodemus. The tremendous panache of this literary account is reflected in the following passage, which also closely reflects the iconographic formula of the Bristol panel:

> And behold, suddenly Hades trembled, and the gates of death and the bolts were shattered and the iron bars were broken and fell to the ground, everything was exposed. And Satan remained in the midst and stood confounded and downcast, bound with fetters on his feet. And behold, the Lord Jesus Christ, coming in the brightness of celestial light from on high, compassionate, great, and lowly, carrying a chain in his hand, bound Satan by the neck, and tying his hands behind him dashed him on his back into Tartarus and set his holy foot on his throat.... Then the Lord Jesus, the Saviour of all, kind and gentle, greeted Adam and said to him, 'Peace be to you, Adam, with your children, through immeasurable ages....' Then Adam (and Eve) fell down at the feet of the Lord and then, rising, kissed his hands and shed many tears. And testified to all, 'Behold the hands which fashioned me'.

The Bristol 'Harrowing' pictures this episode. Although the surface of the stone is damaged and discoloured and the limestone carving is worn and broken in parts, the towering image of Christ and the diminutive Adam and Eve on the right of the panel can still be clearly discerned. Christ, bearded and sporting a moustache, carries a cross and appears to be blessing the couple with his right hand. Adam and Eve stretch up their hands, perhaps to hold the base of the cross or to touch the left hand of Christ. The dialogue which closes the passage quoted above is reflected in these gestures. Less easy to see are the details at the bottom of the panel. Here on the right, a monster's head, its mouth gaping open, provides the support upon which Adam and Eve stand. To the left a sprawling figure lies with arms manacled, legs splayed out up the sides of the panel, and head firmly pinioned by Christ's left foot. These details represent the defeated Satan and the mouth of hell.

Close as the panel is to the apocryphal account, this is not to argue for a direct link between the two. By the Romanesque period, a rich tradition associated with Christ's Harrowing of Hell had built up both in art and literature. The story had been retold many times, including a lengthy version in the late Anglo-Saxon poem 'Christ and Satan'. These narratives place the event chronologically between the Crucifixion and the Resurrection when, on Easter Saturday, Christ journeyed into the underworld to release all those souls imprisoned there since the Fall. The episode would have reached its widest audience through its inclusion in the version of the creed known as the Apostles' Creed, which dates in its final form from the eighth century. Here the scene is briefly described as 'He descended into Hell'. Beyond the narrative, however, the scene developed a more abstract significance. It became one of the motifs which, along with the Crucifixion/Resurrection sequence, symbolised the triumph of Christ over Death, in which the part of Death is played by the figure prostrate at Christ's feet.

This significance is clear when we turn to the iconographic history of the Harrowing of Hell. In the Byzantine world the image was described not as the 'Harrowing of Hell' but as the *Anastasis,* a word which may be translated as 'raising' or 'resurrection'. Two raisings and two conquests may be implied from this title. First, Christ himself in his resurrection is triumphant over death, and secondly in raising Adam and Eve and their descendants from the clutches of hell, they too are granted eternal life. The image therefore has references both to the Resurrection and to Redemption. Similarly, the iconographic family to which this type of image belongs corroborates the reading of this image as one that represents the conquest of evil and death. Other types that include the motif of a righteous figure fighting and conquering a monster include 'Christ treading the Beasts', numerous saints fighting with dragons, and a conventional funerary motif in which the deceased is shown with a serpent beneath his feet signifying his aspirations for eternal life. Finally, the context of many surviving medieval Harrowing of Hell images reinforces this reading. Whilst the motif frequently, and perhaps especially in psalter illustrations, is flanked by scenes of the Passion and Resurrection, there are a number of examples where it appears in an actual or implied Last Judgement context: the sculptures at Lincoln and Hereford Cathedrals, for example, and the 'Doom' painting at Chaldon in Surrey. The redemptive reading makes sense here because the motif thereby offers hope to the faithful to counter their fear of damnation. For contemporaries, therefore, the image would have had its own intrinsic meaning as well as simply representing an episode in a narrative.

The specific scene of the 'Harrowing' or 'Descent into Hell' had developed in the early Christian Roman and Byzantine churches, two early eighth century examples surviving, for instance, in the church of Sta Maria Antiqua in Rome. Both Greek and Latin types showed Christ releasing Adam and Eve from Hell. There are, however, important variations between the two. The Byzantine *Anastasis* tends to include prominently amongst the saved two or three Old Testament kings and the figure of John the Baptist, whose own death preceded that of Christ's, so denying him too the immediate fruits of Redemption. Liberally scattered over the foreground of this group of images are locks and hinges and broken doors signifying the tearing down of the gates of hell. The western version, on the other hand, evolved different peripheral motifs. Adam and Eve, for instance, tend to be dressed with the other figures naked. While the doors of hell are often depicted as a monster's gaping maw from as early as the eighth century, the entrance may also be represented in this way, as in the Bristol panel. As we have seen, the representation of death and hell as a monster was commonplace in Christian and also in classical Roman art.

It may also be that the development of the hell-mouth was influenced by the description of the monster Leviathan in the Old Testament. This creature, spitting out smoke and flames, was seen by theologians of the Middle Ages as a type for the infernal underworld. A mid-twelfth century German triptych, now in the Victoria and Albert Museum in London, illustrates Leviathan as a type for Hell and the two types of entrance into the infernal regions. A central image of the 'Harrowing' is flanked by two Old Testament types. The first shows the fishing of Leviathan and the inscription tells us that Christ is the fish-hook going down into the monster's mouth to conquer Hell. The second shows Samson carrying off the gates of Gaza, so in this type reference is made to the doors of Hell rather than to the mouth. The iconography involving doors and the monster's mouth was therefore well grounded in the theological commentaries of the Middle Ages. A final distinction between the Byzantine type in comparison with its western counterpart is concerned with the posture of Christ. The Greek world developed early on a composition whereby Christ is shown striding away from Hell as he pulls Adam and Eve after him. In the west, the earliest examples show Christ turning to face Adam and Eve as they emerge from the monster's jaws.

These eastern and western formulae, of course, only represent general trends, and there was considerable influence from the Byzantine world on some western versions of the image. In England, too, the ultimate influence of Greek models can be seen in perhaps the earliest surviving British representation of the scene. The Harley Psalter, in the British Library, was copied by the monks of Christchurch Priory, Canterbury, around 1000. It was modelled on a ninth century French psalter that had come into their possession, now known as the Utrecht Psalter. The copy is superficially close, but there is variance in details. On folio 71v of the Canterbury manuscript a small scene shows Christ rescuing souls from hell. In the French original, Christ faces the souls, following the western convention. In the Canterbury copy he turns away from them in the Greek way. It is intriguing to wonder why the eleventh century English artist chose to deviate from the original in this detail. Again, when in twelfth century Lincoln a frieze was carved to ornament the west front of the cathedral, the scene of the Harrowing included John the Baptist standing next to Christ as he rescued souls from the hell-mouth, another echo from the Byzantine world.

An early British example of the traditional western type of the image appears in a mid-eleventh century manuscript, the so-called Tiberius Psalter in the British Library. Iconographically, this is close to the Bristol panel in the details of the hell-mouth, the naked Adam and Eve and the posture of Christ. The survival of this, alongside the Harley Psalter detail, demonstrates that, by the middle of the century, English artists had access to a rich source of models for images of the Harrowing of Hell. When considering the dating of the sculpture it would therefore be feasible, on iconographic grounds, to place it in the eleventh century, although other monumental examples, as opposed to manuscript illuminations, do not survive earlier than the twelfth century. Stylistically a number of scholars, amongst them Gardiner, Zarnecki, Stone and Smith, have recognised similarities between the panel and other British images of the eleventh century in both manuscripts and sculptures. The roped hair, the hunched left shoulder, the buoyant stance of Christ, the trapezoidal shape and the scooping out technique used by the sculptor can all be seen in other extant examples of pre-Conquest Anglo-Saxon sculpture. In terms of medium, too, an early date is possible. There was a well-established school of monumental sculptors in Anglo-Saxon England at periods dating from at least the seventh century, at Reculver in Kent, for example. The Ruthwell cross in Galloway, for instance, perhaps dating from the ninth century, features a large figure of Christ triumphant over the Beasts, a theme which has much in common with the Harrowing of Hell. A work of the scale and ambition of the Bristol panel would not therefore be out of place in a British eleventh century context.

Dating such a unique and contextually isolated carving is, however, fraught with problems. Arguments can also inevitably be advanced in support of a later twelfth century date. Turning again to style, comparisons that have been made with manuscript drawings are hazardous because of the contrasting nature of the media in relation to scale, technique and materials. When considering the Bristol panel alongside more securely dated Anglo-Saxon sculptures, some of its features seem to compare and others do not. The carving of Christ at Beverston in Gloucestershire with which the Bristol example has been previously compared is a much more slight, floating figure. It features the flicking drapery typical of the so-called 'Winchester' style and appears to be beardless, which is in keeping with late Anglo-Saxon iconography, itself so influenced by the ninth century Carolingian schools. By contrast the overall solidity of the outline of the figure of the Bristol Christ, and the linearity of the draperies, can also be found in English sculpture of the twelfth century. A comparison may be made with a limestone figure of St Paul dated about 1160, from the Augustinian Priory of Ivychurch in Wiltshire. Whilst it may be said that the Bristol Christ sports a Winchester flick at his heel, it is a diffident affair and can also be cited in later Romanesque figure sculpture. The roped hair, although appearing in the Anglo-Saxon period, is more prevalent later. From the point of view of style, scale, medium and technique, the arguments are therefore strong for the eleventh century, but a later twelfth century dating cannot be ruled out.

Iconographically, a stronger case may perhaps be made for the later date. From the eleventh century we have a small detail of a Harrowing of Hell from a Canterbury Psalter of *c*.1000 and a mid-century full-page miniature from a Winchester Psalter. No monumental examples survive. By contrast, there is a group still extant from the twelfth century, of which the largest number survive in the south-western quarter of the country at Shobdon and Eardisley, Herefordshire; Hereford Cathedral; Quenington and South Cerney, Gloucestershire; and Billesley, Warwickshire, for example. Of these the Hereford Cathedral capital is the earliest, dating to the second decade of the twelfth century. Like the Lincoln Cathedral frieze and corresponding Harrowing scenes in twelfth-century English wall painting, it is set in a Judgement context. Compositionally it is the most similar in the group to the Bristol panel. The Gloucestershire group, of which the dating is controversial but probably no later than the 1130s, shows the scene in partnership with an image of Christ glorified. At South Cerney the images appear together and at Quenington the 'Harrowing' is on the north tympanum and the glorified image, this time an early example of Christ in Majesty crowning the Virgin, is on the south. Shobdon, Billesley and Eardisley are all products of the so-called Herefordshire School and date from the middle decades of the century. The Harrowing at Shobdon, the earliest of the group but now detached from its original setting, was similarly arranged to the one at Quenington, on the north tympanum balanced by a glorified Majesty on the south. Compositionally, however, it is quite different from the earlier English examples. It is perhaps worth noting that Shobdon had close links with the founding of the priory at Bristol and was itself the site of the first Augustinian community founded in England from St Victoire in Paris, the mother house also eventually of Bristol. At Eardisley the scene appears on a font, whilst at Billesley the Harrowing is only a fragment but, like Eardisley, shows Christ in the Greek manner walking away from the souls liberated from hell. It may be that the Bristol Harrowing stood as an early prototype for these twelfth century examples. Given the extreme fragmentary nature of the surviving evidence, no definitive conclusion can be reached, but certainly it can be said that, as a monumental scheme, the scene enjoyed some popularity in the twelfth century within a 50-mile radius of Bristol.

This review of the other surviving twelfth-century examples of the Harrowing of Hell in monumental sculpture can help to build up a possible context for our panel. Although it is possible that the image was conceived to stand iconographically alone, even its spatial context would have located its meaning for contemporaries. Whether it stood at a liminal place like the eighth-century Harrowings at Sta Maria Antiqua or whether it was placed outside, perhaps in a cemetery, carved on a cross, would qualify the way it was read. The twelfth-century examples surveyed above, however, were not carved in isolation and all have an iconographic context. As we have seen, the Harrowings appear in the context of Baptism and Judgement and perhaps, in the case of South Cerney and Shobdon, as the redeeming face of God. On the other hand, in the context of manuscript illumination the Harrowing is most often set in a Passion sequence. How may our panel have been visually related with other images?

This brings us back to the question with which we started. What was the original function of the Bristol Harrowing of Hell? Let us first of all assume the probability that the sculpture pre-dates the abbey building of the twelfth century, and that it was made for this site and not, for an unknown reason, brought from elsewhere. It should be noted that the stone itself is not local limestone, although that does not preclude the carving being made for this site. Smith, who tentatively supported a late Anglo-Saxon dating, suggested

that it may once have adorned St Jordan's chapel which formerly stood in the cemetery to the north of the present Cathedral, and which was later recorded as being an ancient site of worship commemorating one of the followers of St Augustine of Canterbury. Certainly late Saxon sculpture of this scale survives in another small chapel in the area at St Lawrence, Bradford-upon-Avon. Its shape suggests the shaft of a cross, and another possibility is perhaps to imagine it as part of a larger composition destined to stand in the churchyard in the great tradition of Anglo-Saxon standing crosses. A similar theme had been used on the great Ruthwell cross. More locally, late Anglo-Saxon fragments from

25 Romanesque archway by R.H. Grimm

26 The same archway in 1999, now part of the Cathedral School

standing crosses survive at Codford, Wiltshire, and Congresbury, Somerset, where one face is carved with an image of Christ blessing and holding a cross-staff in his hand, and therefore not dissimilar to the Bristol Christ. A shaft from a mid-eleventh century cross at Shelford in Nottinghamshire demonstrates a carving technique of scooping-out similar to the Bristol example. Given the iconographic context of the Harrowing which we have considered at other sites, and the thematic programmes with which crosses, monumental and otherwise, were adorned in the early Middle Ages, it is possible that the Bristol panel originally formed part of such an object. Again, there are problems with this theory. First, the Bristol panel is only carved on one side and so, if it were part of a cross, it was probably not free-standing. Secondly, the tapering of the sides is slight, and so would have only fitted into part of a massive composition, possibly too large to be feasible.

To speculate on the sculpture once ornamenting the abbey church itself would be to accept the theory that the sculpture was put in the chapter house floor only when the level was raised in the eighteenth century. This would make the Bristol Harrowing a little later in date than the other examples in the twelfth century group. It is also possible that in looking at the panel, a piece apparently discarded at some point in its history, we are witnessing a sculpture set aside not because it had become unfashionable or because it had become unpalatable to a later generation of the faithful, but because it was never finished. The rough-hewn frame, the lack of an architectonic framework, the smooth untreated surfaces of all the figures in the composition except for that of Christ, may suggest this as another theory to explain the enigma of the Bristol Harrowing of Hell.

The twelfth-century Abbey

The Harrowing of Hell is now displayed supported by a pair of Romanesque capitals, which from their size and arrangement may once have formed part of the twelfth century cloister of the abbey church. Twinned capitals on this scale once adorned the Romanesque cloister at Westminster Abbey, and can still be seen in the Romanesque cloister at Moissac in south-west France. The church and related abbey buildings founded by Fitzharding survive as fragments like these, with the exception of the chapter house and abbey gatehouse. To form a definitive picture of the original abbey based on such evidence is not possible, but a close approximation can perhaps be reached by combining these fragments with documentary accounts and results from archaeological investigations.

The first challenge faced by the twelfth-century builders was how to build this large complex of buildings on such a precipitous site. Modern land levelling and the built-up nature of the area now disguise the fact that the church was originally balanced on the edge of ground which dropped from north to south and increasingly from east to west too, as it stretched down towards the river to its south. Creation of a viable platform for the new buildings would in itself have been a mighty task, and also had a bearing on the subsequent layout of the abbey. This appears to have radiated from a cloister about 28m^2 at the heart of the conventual buildings. On the east side, south of the transept, the chapter house was constructed. Its position slightly deviates from the usual arrangement whereby the slype would run between the transept and chapter house. Here, however, the slype, a passageway from the cloister to the abbey cemetery, runs south of the chapter house which directly abuts on to the church. Leading up from within the south transept, a flight of stairs can still be seen which ran up to a passage above the chapter house vestibule and so into the canons' dorter south of the slype. Via this route, the canons could rise from their beds during sleeping hours and walk directly to the church to attend the night offices. On the site of the dorter the land begins to fall away steeply, and here to the south-east a vaulted undercroft of the twelfth century still survives well below the ground level of the former cemetery area to its north. Further to the south and west, later buildings have obscured the original Romanesque layout of the abbey, but at the south-western corner of the present complex of Cathedral and School, two Romanesque doorways can still be seen which once led to the abbot's lodgings. As one walks through these doorways the wall to the left, formerly part of the abbey guest house, also dates from the twelfth century. The east wall of this building still retains some blocked up Romanesque windows. Finally, the imposing gatehouse, due-west of the church door, encloses within its structure two highly-decorated twelfth-century entrance portals, so the abbey still shows its original Romanesque face to the world, even if little twelfth-century work now survives behind it.

The Romanesque Church

Our present knowledge of the twelfth-century abbey church of St Augustine owes much to the investigations of two former cathedral architects: E.W. Godwin, who published his findings in 1863 prior to the rebuilding of the nave, and Roland Paul, whose article on the Romanesque building appeared in 1912 after the new nave had been completed. No major discoveries have been made since then to dramatically revise the conclusions which they reached, and even these, though soundly based on the available evidence, are not definitive. It seems the church was built from local red Brandon Hill stone; this can still be seen in the Romanesque gable of the south transept, where an original round-headed window appears above the later Perpendicular window faced in grey Dundry freestone, which was used for the later Gothic parts of the building. The redness of the stone would not, however, have been evident to the onlooker of the twelfth century because, as Godwin reported in 1850, it would have been plastered-over inside and out making the church appear almost white. This was a customary practice of the period, perhaps to disguise the rough cutting of masonry or to hide poor building materials. The Romanesque parts of St Alban's Cathedral in Hertfordshire, built from brick and flint, still retain their plaster coats inside the building, whilst pilgrims, we are told, sought the 'white tower' on the hill on the last lap of their journey to the shrine of the English protomartyr. There may be practical as well as symbolic implications in the oft-quoted remark of the eleventh-century monk, Raoul Glaber, who described the wave of church building in the wake of the first millennium in terms of the land being dressed anew in a 'gleaming white robe of churches' (*candidum ecclesiarum vestem*).

The average thickness of the walls of St Augustine's were about 5ft (1.5m). Paul calculated that the overall length of the Romanesque church must have been about 66m from east to west and about 17m wide, with a transept nearly 34m from north to south and about 9m wide. An early visual record of the building appears on the seal of Abbot John who ruled over the community from 1196-1215. This shows a church viewed from the south with round-headed windows in the aisle and clerestory and two bold towers attached to the transept. The seal probably raises more problems than it solves, and certainly cannot be relied upon to be accurate in all its details. First, it implies a nave aisle. Godwin and Paul both assume an aisle, probably narrower than the present one, and leaving a central vessel then, as now, of about 10m width. Street, who designed the present nave, noted in a letter of 1869 that, during preparation of the site for the new building: 'A continuous (foundation) wall was found on each side of the nave giving the impression that, at some date, a nave without aisles existed'. Although archaeologists currently do not acknowledge this evidence as definitively proving that the church originally had no nave aisle, it has been observed that English Augustinian churches of the twelfth century were not infrequently aisle-less — Porchester in Hampshire, Dorchester in Oxon, Wigmore in Herefordshire, and Lilleshall in Shropshire, being four such examples.

Secondly, the seal suggests transept towers, though they may be simply a rather exaggerated sketch of staircase towers such as those which still abut the Romanesque transept at Canterbury Cathedral. The existing twelfth-century masonry in the south transept wall which includes pilaster buttresses at the angles does not suggest that towers were originally situated at these corners, though we can be more certain about a Romanesque crossing tower since the piers which support the present tower appear to have been cut back from the original twelfth-century piers which were cruciform with attached shafts at the end of each arm. The tower may not have been high — Godwin envisaged a squat construction surmounted by a pyramidal wooden roof — but the stoutness of the crossing piers suggests some extra load at this point. A pair of belfry towers may have framed the west end as William Wyrcester describes in his fifteenth century *Itinerarium,* which Paul suggested stood proud of the aisles behind them. Godwin and Norris refer to a Galilee chapel running along the entire west end of the Norman nave in front of the two belfries. This arrangement was characteristic of Cistercian churches in the twelfth century and can still be seen at Pontigny in Burgundy and at Fountains in Yorkshire.

The seal provides a good starting-point for speculation on the original appearance of St Augustine's. Street's investigations prior to the rebuilding of the nave give more precise measurements and offer more detailed information with regard to the Romanesque nave. This, he concluded, was made up of five bays in addition to a western bay flanked by the towers. The piers were spaced 18ft (5.5m) from centre to centre. Apart from the west doors he suggested a north door in approximately the same position as that occupied by the present north door, which would provide the means of access to the church from the outside. Doors from the nave into the cloister were probably positioned opposite the north door and another further east. Doors in these positions can still be seen at Ely Cathedral and can be discerned in the Romanesque fabric of the nave at Winchester.

The elevation of the nave, although the detail now eludes us, would almost certainly have been tripartite in the Anglo-Norman manner, assuming the building had aisles. An idea of a more or less contemporary elevation in an Augustinian church can still be seen to north and south of the choir of St Bartholomew the Great in Smithfield, London. In his 1863 article Godwin illustrated a capital, one of a pair which came from the original nave. The capital, foliated at the corners, is an elaborate version of what may be called a stepped trefoil capital, an early example of which survives from the cloisters of Reading Abbey. The illustrated face in Godwin's article is identical to certain capitals that appear in the gatehouse and the chapter house, and may suggest that work on the construction of the nave coincided with the building of these two structures. This type of decorated capital was widely distributed in the late Romanesque world, appearing for instance, in the nave of the twelfth-century parish church of Barneville on the Cotentin peninsula in Normandy.

Moving eastwards, it appears that the plan of the Romanesque transept has not been changed in subsequent rebuildings, although it is possible that apsidal chapels once extended eastwards both on the north and south sides, to be later replaced by the Early English Elder Lady Chapel and the Decorated Newton Chapel. From outside the north transept, the pilaster buttresses of the Romanesque building can be seen both beneath the later Gothic buttress added to reinforce the walls when the transepts were vaulted in the late Middle Ages, and rising up on the east wall above the roof level of the Elder Lady Chapel. More evidence survives in the south transept, where similar twelfth-century buttressing can still be seen in the south-west corner and where the Romanesque gable window already mentioned is set into a rough surround of Brandon Hill stone. On either side of this window the marks of the steep pitch of the original roof are just visible. The original height of the building may also be indicated on the inside of the transept where a Romanesque corbel survives on the wall in the south-west corner. Here too a small twelfth-century window survives above the arch to the Newton Chapel in the east wall. It serves to remind us of the subdued lighting of the original building, quite unlike the bright quality of the present interior lit by the massive perpendicular window of the fifteenth century. Godwin, in his speculative reconstruction of the original building, suggested three windows in a row below the south gable of the transept. A second row would not have been possible because of the proximity of the chapter house. The north transept may have had two rows of windows, perhaps appearing similar to the roughly contemporary fenestration of the transept at Romsey Abbey in Hampshire, where the greater height of the wall allows space for three rows of two windows. Godwin's and Paul's theories concerning the elevation of the original church cannot, of course, be substantiated, but their drawings do convey one of the abiding characteristics of architecture of this period: the dominance of mass over space.

While the rebuilding of the nave led to a few discoveries concerning the original fabric, the arrangement of the Romanesque east end is more elusive, since archaeological investigation of this part of the church has been necessarily limited. It is, however, generally agreed that the original choir was situated underneath the crossing tower and that the church extended three bays east of the crossing and was flanked by aisles of two bays each. The base of a rectangular pier found in 1894 just north of the present choir may mark the junction of the first and second bays of the arcade separating the chancel from the aisle. It provides a convenient marker for the calculation of the proportions of this part of the building. Like its Gothic successor it seems that the east end was not apsidal and that both chancel and aisles culminated in flat walls. This arrangement was not

uncommon in late English Romanesque, appearing also, for instance, at Sarum II and probably at Romsey. It is not, however, typical of Austin houses which, as J.F. Hodgson demonstrated, did not for the most part follow any characteristic patterns, unlike contemporary Cistercian foundations. Issues such as the lighting of the interior, the relative costs of apsidal as opposed to non-apsidal buildings, the availability of building skills, the liturgical use of the apsidal space, and local tradition may all have influenced the decision for this floor plan. Had it survived it may have been instructive to compare the design of St Augustine's with its daughter Victorine house at Keynsham, a community founded by Robert Fitzharding's son, William, in 1173. The two churches may well have displayed a family likeness. Godwin suggested altars at the east end of both chancel aisles and a *via processionum* following around the east end of the church which would have perambulated the choir and sanctuary. This area was probably surrounded by a screen with the high altar at its east end.

28 Chapter house
   detail
29 Chapter house
   detail

There is no evidence that the church was vaulted, which is to be expected in a building that was, after all, of simple design and built from rough local masonry. Smith noted its small scale in comparison with the great Benedictine foundations of the medieval diocese, such as Evesham, Tewkesbury, Gloucester and Pershore. Even amongst Augustinian houses Bristol was not amongst the largest. It was much smaller, for instance, than the abbey at Cirencester, now destroyed. However, as the building work proceeded westward, and especially after 1155 when finances were refreshed through the income from the Berkeley estates newly acquired by Fitzharding, we can imagine more decorative stonework being included in the church design, a development certainly reflected in the exuberant treatment of the chapter house and abbey gatehouse which Godwin suggests were begun at about this time. It is perhaps towards this end of the building that the series of Romanesque corbel heads, now hidden away in a stair well off the north choir aisle, was originally situated. This series of nine carved heads bear the hallmarks of English sculpture towards the middle of the twelfth century, especially in the south-west, and may be compared to similar carvings forming the voussoirs of arches at churches such as Windrush in Gloucestershire, Kilpeck in Herefordshire and Iffley in Oxon. Three in particular are similar to a kind of carved head known as a 'beakhead' in which a beak-like protuberance extends from the grotesque face of a monster and curls round a roll-moulding below it. They appear to have made their earliest fully-developed appearance at Reading Abbey in the 1130s. It is a type which functionally belongs to arches, especially around doorways where an outer order of carved voussoirs frames an inner roll-moulding. Beak-head types could however be used in other contexts such as corbel tables. Smith drew attention to the contemporary and stylistically similar corbel table at Clevedon, a foundation dependent upon St Augustine's.

The chapter house

If the Romanesque church has largely disappeared from view, the chapter house survives as the finest twelfth century building of its kind in the country. It was here that the business of the community was transacted at regular meetings. Though there was seating for 52, it seems unlikely that this number was ever achieved. On major occasions when representatives from dependent churches and the estates were required to be present, the visitors could follow the proceedings through the openings on either side of the door. It was not until 1877 that these openings were glazed. Eighteenth-century prints show a staircase and a fireplace, but the latter was almost certainly a later addition, perhaps at the Reformation. As we have already seen, it was under the floor of the chapter house when it was being restored in 1832 that the Harrowing of Hell stone was found, along with other coffin lids and remains.

The highly textured walls of the chapter house, like a rich lithic fabric, represent a style that stands in stark contrast to the gentler, more refined lines of the Gothic style of the present church. Charged with energy of an almost primitive dynamism, it provided an apt backdrop to the drama of abbey life that was enacted daily within its walls. The precise rules laid out for the chapter meeting in a Victorine monastery can still be savoured today through reference to surviving documents which relate to St Augustine's mother house in Paris. The rules given for the conduct of these meetings are prescriptive in the extreme, described in meticulous detail and leaving no room for improvisation. The meeting is announced by a bell; the canons promptly respond as they gather into a line ordered according to rank; they respectfully acknowledge the abbot as they file past him and display their obeisance before the great crucifix, and then move to their appointed seats.

The meetings then followed this pattern: the date was announced from the lectern, followed by prayers, the benediction from the abbot and a reading from the rule. Prayers on behalf of deceased benefactors and past members of the community were read, the register was called, and then there was the sermon, after which those present who were not canons left; individual duties for the performance of the daily office were then allocated. The final section of the meeting dealt with matters of discipline: those who had committed a fault were invited to confess it, and accusations were made as they were thought to be justified. Punishments involved public beatings in front of the rest of the chapter and were administered by a fellow canon who, it is specified, had not to be of inferior rank to the man undergoing chastisement.

At each point in this account the writer specifies particular phrases which the protagonists have to say, and the precise movements which have to be made. A strict eye is kept on hierarchical propriety so that at no point in the proceedings is any disrespect shown to superiors. One can imagine a meeting of the same or very similar kind being held at the Bristol chapter house in the first decades after its construction. It was a formal and, in places, highly ritualised event which confirmed respect for the social order and traditions of the community and due punishment of any behaviour which might pose a threat to it.

Except for the sedilia that line the walls, nothing now survives in the chapter house to indicate its original usage. From the Parisian account we perhaps should imagine both a lectern and a crucifix in the room as part of its original furnishings. We can also include in our mental picture a coloured interior. The walls and vault are not only sculpturally ornate but were once further adorned with polychromy. Investigations carried out in the late 1980s revealed traces of red and a darker colour as well as white. Given the pervasiveness of the sculptural decoration, there is little room for figurative painting except, perhaps, on the vault. The Bristol walls do not have the space to allow for an elaborate didactic scheme such as the one formerly painted round the walls of the twelfth-century chapter house at Worcester depicting New Testament scenes and their types from the Old Testament. At Worcester the backs of the sedilia still retain traces of painted drapery. This economic alternative to the use of real textiles is commonly found in twelfth-century wall-painting, draping, for instance, the dado of the painted walls at Clayton and Hardham in Sussex, and imitating a hanging behind an altar in the Galilee Chapel in Durham. Can we imagine such a device used to decorate the backs of the canons' sedilia at St Augustine's?

Like the medieval canons, we approach the chapter house today through the east cloister walk and via an ante-room three bays wide and two deep. The ante-room is lower than the chapter house itself because above it runs the passage from the dorter to the night stairs where recently an original twelfth-century wooden door has been discovered, and where two small Romanesque windows are still pierced in the exterior wall. Both ante-room and chapter house are faced by finely cut ashlar masonry. The red Brandon Hill stone behind can still be seen above the level of the ashlar at the entrance to the ante-room. This room shows its transitional character architecturally in the employment of both round and pointed arches in its vault, the former running from north to south and the latter from east to west. In the middle decades of the twelfth century the employment of pointed arches was still relatively new in English architecture. Their use here ideally solves the problem raised when bays are rectangular in shape. The semicircle supporting the long side of the bay would have to have been awkwardly stilted were that shape also to be used to support the short side. A pointed arch, on the other hand, is more flexible in the way its width can be adapted to fit a wide range of spaces. A grander contemporary example in an Augustinian context can be seen in the supports of the crossing tower of St Bartholomew the Great in London, which employ two round and two pointed arches.

The ante-room is entered through a triple arched front, a typical arrangement for this situation which can also be seen, for instance, at Fountains Abbey in Yorkshire and at the late twelfth century Augustinian foundation of Haughmond in Shropshire. There are sedilia on the north and south walls and a stone bench running along the east side, indicating the use of this space as a lobby for those waiting for admission to the chapter house. The decoration is similar in style to that of the chapter house but less exuberant and, in the same way, there is a quadripartite ribbed vault, although too small in scale to necessitate transverse arches. The ribs have soffits decorated with beading, and broad roll mouldings, and are supported in the centre by free-standing square piers with attached shafts. On the centre of each side wall two ribs spring from one scalloped capital supported by a spindly shaft forming the jamb between a pair of sedilia. The intersection of the ribs in the western bays are masked by foliate and knot bosses.

Inevitably over the centuries some of the stonework has had to be recut or replaced, but enough original work survives to show that these restorations were carried out fully in sympathy with the twelfth-century work. In the chapter house itself more dramatic changes have been effected mostly because of its reorganisation and some restructuring for use as a library in the eighteenth century, and as a result of the severe damage done to the east end in the Bristol Riots of 1831. The changes have left some questions still unanswered concerning the appearance of the original building. The main controversy centres on the twelfth-century floor-plan. The earliest reference to the dimensions of the building appear in William Wyrcestre's *Itinerarium* of the late fifteenth century in which the building is described as being three times as long as wide, measuring about 74ft (22.5m) by about 25ft (7.5m). Even if the ante-room is included the present chapter house would still not be this length. The question therefore emerges to what extent the east end was remodelled in the nineteenth-century repairs or perhaps even prior to that. There are three possibilities: first, that there was originally a third rectangular bay to the east, secondly that the east end terminated in an apse instead of a third bay, and thirdly that Wyrcestre's measurements were inaccurate and that the original floor-plan corresponded closely to the present one. The post-Reformation history of the building does not really begin until the late seventeenth century, when reference is made to the building being 'out of repair and not fit to talk of business or discourse there'. This process of abandonment may have begun in the wake of Bristol's surrender to Fairfax in 1645. Whether, in the sixteenth century, any changes were made to the chapter house after the foundation was raised to cathedral status, we do not know.

In 1714, the building was adapted for use as a library. The floor was raised about a metre, two large sash windows being inserted into the east end and a small one on the south. A fireplace was also installed on the south side. These features are recorded in Lyson's engraving of 1804, by Skelton in 1825, and again by Winkles in 1838. However, at some point in the post-riot restorations they were removed, which would have entailed considerable restructuring of the south-west wall of the chapter house where they were located. Browne Willis in 1727 describes a circular Romanesque window in the east wall of the chapter house that suggests an original flat termination. Certainly there were precedents in twelfth-century Bristol for circular windows. The Benedictine priory church of St James founded in 1129 and completed by 1147 had such a window in the gable of its west front, recorded in Skelton's early nineteenth century etching and which can still be seen in the design of the present building which is now much restored. In Storer's history of the Cathedral written in 1814 a floor-plan of the Chapter house shows a flat east end. An engraving in J. Britton's *History and Antiquities of the Abbey and Cathedral Church of Bristol* of 1830 again shows a flat east end, but articulated by a large Gothic arch. Could this argue for a re-modelling in the Gothic period? In the 1880s J.P. Norris arranged an excavation of the area beyond the present east end. Nothing was found, and it was then presumed that there had never been a further extension to the east. However, in 1901 H. Massé proposed that an excavation looking for an eastern bay may have missed evidence of an eastern apse. In 1912 Roland Paul supported this theory.

The evidence from these commentators, especially from those writing before the riots, rather points to the likelihood that the chapter house did not have an apse, at least not by the post-medieval period, and the archaeological investigations indicate no work beyond the existing east bay. Looking at comparative evidence from extant twelfth-century chapter houses, it appears that quite a variety of floor-plans were adopted for this purpose. Worcester is polygonal, Durham is apsidal and Rochester is rectangular. Amongst the solely monastic, as opposed to cathedral, chapter houses, the Cluniac Much Wenlock in Shropshire is rectangular. In terms of the decoration applied to its walls, this building is probably the closest in style to Bristol. Repton in Derbyshire, an Augustinian house, is rectangular, and Christchurch, Oxford, is also Augustinian, although the present chapter house dating from the thirteenth century (the entrance is late Romanesque) is the same shape. On the other hand the late twelfth century chapter house of the Augustinian foundation at Kenilworth in Warwickshire was apsidal. Smith draws attention to the case of the Cluniac chapter house at Castle Acre in Norfolk. He notes that this too was apsidal in the twelfth century but was modified in the first half of the fourteenth century to produce a flat east end pierced with a large window. Reverting to the engraving in Britton's book, he wonders whether the large Gothic window illustrated there was inserted during the Perpendicular period, when much work was done on the conventual buildings at Bristol, at the same time doing away with the apse. If William Wyrcestre, who died in the 1480s, took his measurements of the building before this modification was effected, then the excessive length he registers could be explained by the existence of a

Romanesque apse. Browne Willis' reference to the round window in the east wall perhaps conflicts with this theory and looking at the spirit of Britton's engraving, the Romanticism of the composition raises doubts about its absolute accuracy with regard to architectural detail. Clearly the conundrum relating to the original design of the east end must remain unanswered. However, this survey of the available evidence does perhaps suggest that the chapter house did not have a third rectangular bay and that, if it did once have an apse, it had probably been removed by the Reformation.

On entering the chapter house today, the view east reveals the restored facing wall, rebuilt after the Bristol riots, which terminates a room remarkable for the richness of its late Romanesque geometric sculptural decoration. The quadripartite ribbed vault rises to a height of about 25ft (7.5m), and the two bays are divided by a broad transverse arch. On each side of the room are 20 sedilia, and further seats for the canons would have ranged along the original east wall — adequate seating for a community that probably never numbered more than thirty, although visitors, estate officers and resident servants of the abbey would have inflated that figure considerably. A tenuous symmetry in the overall impact of the design soon breaks down on closer inspection. The diagonal ribs of the vault are decorated with chevron in one direction and chevron with a central hexagonal foliate design in the other. Chevron is the basic motif of the transverse rib too, elaborated by nailhead. The intersection of the ribs is marked by simple bosses of different designs and similar to those which appear in the ante-room and in the abbey gatehouse. Their flatness of execution is reminiscent of figured twelfth-century bosses at Kempley in Herefordshire and Elkstone in Gloucestershire. A decade or so later, St Augustine's daughter house at Keynsham was to employ bosses to mask the intersection of ribs which were much more Gothic in spirit — deeply undercut and more fleshy in style. We cannot be sure now where these bosses were once employed, since the building they adorned no longer exists, but Zarnecki suggests the chapter house as a possible location.

The north and south walls are each composed of two bays, their upper parts based on woven diaper, vertical or horizontal chevron patterns. These patterns change along the walls unpredictably and almost imperceptibly. The decoration on the upper part of the north-west section of wall, for instance, drifts from diaper into nailhead chevron as it moves upwards. Whilst the lower border of the north-west wall terminates in jagged points which float above the tops of the intersecting arcading below, the points on the border of the corresponding part on the north-east wall are flattened against the arches.

Above the sedilia the continuous intersecting arcading runs the length of both walls. As elsewhere in the chapter house, the verticals of the different registers of decoration do not correspond, so giving the overall effect of a horizontally stretching design. Here the dominating motifs are spirals with nailhead borders. Spiral columns of many varieties appear in Romanesque architecture throughout Europe — in the Monreale cloisters in Sicily, the cloisters at Santo Domingo de Silos in Northern Spain, and the west front of St Lazare in Avallon in Burgundy, for instance. In England they survive in the eighth-century Anglo-Saxon crypt at Repton, and famously amongst the giant drum piers of the nave at Durham. Smith noted a nailhead spiral column decorating the scene between the priest and Aelgyfa in the eleventh-century Bayeux Tapestry. The spirals at Bristol are used on a miniature scale and carved into the masonry.

The row of pointed arches, a natural result of intersecting semi-circles, are outlined by spirals, while the semi-circles are edged with nailhead. The supporting columns alternate between plain and spiral, and the intervening row of capitals demonstrate a variety of designs, many of which are based on the scalloped form. Amongst these a few — the fourth and ninth from the west on the north side and the ninth from the west on the south side — are identical to some which still decorate the great abbey gatehouse which Godwin assumes to be contemporary with the chapter room. Halfway along each side, a flat buttress flanked by spiral shafts supporting scalloped capitals provides the central springers for the vault ribs. A spiral string-course underlines the arcading, and below, the sedilia, hollowed back into the ashlar, are plainly conceived framed by a simple roll-moulding supported by plain jambs. The seats appear to be short on leg room because the floor, although lowered again in the nineteenth-century restorations, is still not back to its original twelfth-century level.

The west wall pursues the theme of intersecting arcading. The top row, chevron on the jambs, glides into a spiral motif over the arches. The architectonic elements of capital and plinth do not appear and this section, like the upper walls to north and south in the chapter house, is simply an exercise in linear ornamentation. This may arise from the awkward shape into which the arcading has to fit, which would not easily accommodate capital and plinth. This is a type of arcading which can also be seen elsewhere in the area in buildings dating from about this time; the west front of Malmesbury Abbey, for example. These features are resumed in the bottom row of arcading which is treated similarly to that on the north and south walls. An interesting deviation can be seen, however, on the central shaft above the door where the spiralling changes direction temporarily half way down. This may be a deliberate ploy on the part of the twelfth-century mason to emphasise the central point in the wall, or a clumsy error on the part of a later restorer.

The door flanked by two windows is set below a nailhead spiral string-course. The decorated hood-moulds which frame them rise up into the string-course, pushing against it and giving a sense of muscular energy to the design. Beneath sturdy roll-mouldings the space is divided into two subsidiary windows below a solid tympanum. The central shaft between the windows is of a dark shiny material, a Purbeck 'marble', or close equivalent. This material, which is not a marble at all but a limestone crammed with fossil remains, became very fashionable in English architecture between the mid-twelfth and mid-thirteenth century. Its use was primarily decorative — a means of punctuating the design by introducing a contrasting colour into the masonry. It was employed in the Galilee Chapel at Durham Cathedral constructed between 1170 and 1175, but at Bristol it makes a still earlier appearance. It would be interesting to know to what extent Purbeck marble featured in the design of the Romanesque nave.

When Leversage was writing in the mid-nineteenth century he noted that these windows had been, until recently, blocked up — a curious decision presumably taken by the eighteenth-century restorers who, after all, were adapting the chapter house for use as a library. One would therefore assume that maximal lighting would have been desirable. However, given that the floor was at the same time raised more than a metre, these windows, for over a hundred years, would only have been good to illuminate people's feet! He also comments on the metal grilles, which he maintains date from the Middle Ages. If so, then this would imply that the windows were originally glazed and so required the protection of metal stanchions. Alternatively they may have simply been shuttered or left open to the air.

Fragments from the monastic buildings

With the exception of the abbey gatehouse, many of the remaining pieces from the Romanesque conventual buildings are so fragmented and de-contextualised that little can be deduced from them. Their rich decoration does however testify to the presence at Bristol of considerable areas of late Romanesque monastic building in stone which was treated to expansive, and expensive, sculptural embellishment. Some of the best examples are set into the stairwell leading up to the area once occupied by the dorter. Here the familiar repertory of geometric designs, already seen in the chapter house and the abbey gatehouse, can be discerned in fragmentary form with further examples displayed on the window-sills outside the offices on the upper storey.

A series of three twelfth-century doorways also survive on the east side of the cloister south of the chapter house. One of them is now situated at the bottom of the stairs just mentioned, whilst another adjacent to it leads into a passage which comes out into the cemetery to the south-east of the church. It is simple in design, but the arch facing the cemetery is modelled into three orders and includes some nailhead ornament. A third door from the cloister, further south, has a sub-arch supported by half shafts with heavily scalloped capitals. A fourth arch now apparently reset on the exterior of the south wall of the chapter house is crowned with a flat arch upon which chevron ornamentation both frames and cuts into a roll moulding. Upon each 'tooth' of the chevron a highly formalised circular floriate decoration appears. The way the teeth fold over the moulding like beaks and the face-like shape of the decoration give this fragment the appearance of an embryonic beakhead.

South-east of the dorter, where the ground level begins to fall away, a more complete feature from the twelfth-century abbey survives in the form of a vaulted undercroft which would once have supported a contemporary superstructure, now disappeared. Lynam suggested that the room may have functioned as the sub-vault to the calefactory. The undercroft is two bays deep and three bays wide measuring approximately 5m by 4m. The groin vaulting and the walls are built from rough Brandon Hill stone that would once have been plastered over. The supporting freestanding columns and scalloped capitals, however, are constructed from ashlar masonry.

Before coming to the abbey gatehouse, a final important feature of the twelfth-century conventual buildings can still be seen at the south-west corner of the monastic complex. The gatehouse to the abbot's lodgings, now known as the Lower Gate, includes two Romanesque archways that Godwin suggested were contemporary with the early building of the church. Although they are less exuberantly decorated than the chapter house and gatehouse, they are nevertheless faced with the same stone, and the motifs with which they are decorated are related to those structures and with the fragments mentioned above. The outer gate has three orders, supported by plain jambs and scalloped capitals. Of the three recessed arches the two inner ones are decorated with chevron, with the outer of the two arranged over two faces of the arch around a moulded spine. The outer arch has a woven design like basket work, a pattern which also appears on the north side of the small arch in the abbey gatehouse. The emulation of textiles in late Romanesque sculpture is relatively common. Similar effects can be seen, for instance, on the Herefordshire fonts at Eardisley and Castle Frome, and an almost identical design survives on a fragment at Brinsop in the same county. A simple low relief chevron band frames the whole. The gate appears smaller now than it would have done originally because of the Perpendicular infill displaying the arms and rebus of Abbot Newland. The eastern arch is simpler, having only one order. The basketwork design appears on the arch that is again supported by scalloped capitals and plain jambs.

The Abbey gatehouse

The entrance into the monastic precinct was marked by an elaborate gatehouse — an architectural statement of the prestige claimed by the community. Such ambitious structures are a common feature of medieval monasteries and still survive at Canterbury, Norwich and St Albans. A fine Romanesque example is recorded which once marked the entrance to the great Benedictine abbey of Bury St Edmunds. The Augustinians were no exception in this and late medieval examples can still be seen at Worksop in Nottinghamshire, St Osyth in Essex and Butley in Suffolk.

The Bristol gatehouse now stands isolated at some distance from the west front of the Cathedral, but originally it would have stood amidst other conventual buildings to east and west. The gatehouse comprises work from a number of different periods. The main vaulted great gate and the smaller, unvaulted postern gate adjoining it appear to belong to the late Romanesque period and are contemporary in style with the chapter house. The upper parts are late Perpendicular and were probably built in the time of Abbot Newland whose roll concludes with a list of all the work he undertook, including the gatehouse. The building has clearly, however, been much restored over the centuries and consequently there have been disagreements among commentators concerning the authenticity of certain parts of the building. Britton in the early nineteenth century and Massé a century later felt that the pristine nature of the Romanesque carved work, apparently exposed to the air for centuries, indicated that it must have undergone a major restoration since the twelfth century. Smith, in his investigations of the gatehouse, noted a number of stones bearing mason's marks on the arcading within the gateway 'as if the building had been taken to pieces after numbering each stone and then reassembled'. One of the capitals, he noted, bore the date 1714. A public debate between Godwin and Street turned on the question of the date of the lower part of the Gatehouse. Godwin claimed it was entirely of the fifteenth century, a sort of Perpendicular exercise in neo-Romanesque, whilst Street supported the view, generally accepted today, that the lower parts of the construction were indeed twelfth century in origin. Certainly major reconstruction is documented in the nineteenth century. Whilst Skelton's view of 1825 shows the original fifteenth-century oriel windows, a Victorian photograph of 1853, now in the Cathedral archives, shows these replaced by sash windows. However, in 1888 the oriels were restored at a cost of £3110.

The nineteenth-century work did not explicitly interfere with the Romanesque parts of the gatehouse and we may presume, despite Godwin's reservations, that the overall design of this part of the structure is authentic. Certainly a number of the motifs employed also appear in the chapter house, as well as in other extant local fragments of late Romanesque sculptural decoration. The nailhead intersecting arcading which appears in both gatehouse and chapter house can be seen, for instance, on a coffin-slab found in St Philip's Church, Bristol. Details were published by Godwin in 1853. The main gate, on the north side, is composed of three orders. The outer order features the arcading to which reference has just been made, and chevron. The arch here flows straight into the jambs, without the intervention of capitals, reminiscent of the arrangement on the west wall of the chapter house. The middle order is composed of a new motif — nailhead bands weaving in and out of two plain parallel bands. This arch rests on capitals decorated with flat palmettes, which are supported by spiralled jambs with nailhead, another feature of the chapter house. Within the great gateway is a two-bay quadripartite ribbed vault. Like the chapter house the diagonal ribs are not treated the same in each bay, but each is imitated in the adjacent bay. To the north, one rib is plain with nailhead running down each side and the other rib has a double moulding that is similarly flanked by nailhead. The same motifs appear again in the south bay but on the opposite diagonals. The thick transverse rib is chevron round three sides with spines running down the edges. The capitals supporting the vaulting ribs are based on a scalloped design. Under a spiralled string course flanked by nailhead, a row of intersecting arches decorated in the same way is incised into the masonry. The architectonic motif thus becomes simply a device for decorating a wall-surface.

The postern gate to the west, though smaller, is equally elaborately decorated on its north face with a woven nailhead motif on its outer order and capitals more luxuriant in design than those on the larger gateway. The inner side of this entrance where a flat Tudor arch is set into the masonry betrays some adaptation in the Perpendicular period. A blocked door in the west side may have given access to a porter's lodge. Paul recorded the presence of an ancient rectangular building here of large proportions which may have included this accommodation. The inside of the gateway is relatively plain in comparison with its neighbour, though a sixteenth-century woodcut suggests that it may once have had a more elaborate interior and a vault.

The south side of the postern gate is plain but the large gateway is even more decorated at this point than the north side both on its inner and outer faces. The heavily moulded arch is elaborated into four orders to the south and is decorated with arches patterned with nailhead diaper work and chevron to the north. The soffit of the arch is patterned in chevron framing a formal foliate design. The chevron theme continues ever more elaborately on the outer face where all the arches rest on scalloped capitals. This side of the large gateway is perhaps a more individual exercise than the other Romanesque parts of the gatehouse. It has unique variations on the chevron theme which are not found elsewhere in the surviving twelfth-century parts of the church and monastery, and a consistent application of capitals between arch and jamb. Could the work here be the creation of a different or even slightly later generation of masons?

It is fitting to finish this section with a question, since this early part of the abbey's architectural history raises so many, and most still unanswered. Whatever the precise details and chronology of the buildings during this period, we can be sure they existed to serve practical needs and to express the spiritual and worldly aspirations of the community for whom they were built. It is hard to imagine the overriding characteristics of these early generations of canons from a modern perspective, but the twelfth century writer Gerald of Wales, in the following passage, gives a contemporary's opinion of the Augustinian order as a whole, the vision it had and the dilemmas it faced:

> The Augustinian canons are more content than any of the others with a humble and modest way of life. They may not be wholly successful in this, but as far as they can they hold in check the urges of ambition. They dwell among secular people, but they avoid as far as possible the temptations of this world. They are certainly in no way notorious for gluttony or drunkenness, and the possibility of incurring public criticism for lechery or evil-living fills them with dread and shame.

At once a subtly critical and slightly idealised commentary, it helps to breathe life into the Romanesque stones of Bristol.

5 Gothic architecture

To enter the nave and look east is to experience a view unique in British cathedral architecture, indeed a vista unique in Europe. Although there are many other hall churches, here the actual design elements are totally different. On account of its relatively modest dimensions and nineteenth-century nave, it has often been overshadowed by larger cathedrals of conventional design. For too long topographical and architectural volumes have tended to grade cathedrals and greater churches into 'big', 'famous', 'middle-rank' and 'the others'; indeed some critics have gone as far as suggesting that hall churches might be excluded from the top rank of Gothic achievement altogether.

With this negative assessment we disagree. The hall church is a significant feature of Gothic architecture. The nave and aisles of such churches are of approximately the same height. In this way, the form gives a sense of increased spaciousness and unity, with the choir and nave more closely related. It was one way of seeking to convey height to a large building. Before considering this notable feature of Bristol, we must consider the history of Gothic architecture as a whole. The Romanesque character has been dealt with in the previous chapter.

The first important alteration to the Romanesque church was made in the early years of the thirteenth century, when the first almost free-standing Lady Chapel was built on the east side of the north transept, rather as at Ely which survives, or Peterborough where it does not. This chapel is attributed to Abbot David (1215-34) who was interred in it, and whose ledger is thought to be the raised stone with head and cross now set in the adjoining transept pavement.

The four bay chapel is of great beauty, both of proportion and detail, only marred by the exposed tufa of the vault (which was formerly plastered, as are the contemporary vaults at Wells). Indeed there is a close connection with that cathedral, as the Abbot of St Augustine's asked the Dean of Wells, between 1218 and 1220, for the loan of his Servant L 'to hew out the seven pillars of wisdom's house, meaning, of course, our chapel of the Blessed Virgin'. As mentioned earlier, 'L' is likely to have been Adam Lock, master mason of Wells until his death in 1229. Lock was in charge of the building of the western section of the Wells nave and appears to not only have been an architectural designer and mason of distinction, but also a man of substance, leaving several houses with land in his will. Certainly the work closely resembles that at Wells, and the lively carving introduced into the spandrels of the wall arcades is superb.

The windows of the chapel have shafts of blue lias — the use of 'marble' was exceedingly popular at this period for lancet windows, triforia etc. and can be seen at Rochester Cathedral, Canterbury, Salisbury, and on the Wells west front, all work of the thirteenth century. Many details of the mouldings and carvings show the link with the work at Wells Cathedral. The east window of the chapel has geometric tracery, probably of around 1275, and because the vaulting has a ridge rib and its bosses are naturalistic and not stiff leaf, it seems that this too was added later, although, of course, originally planned for the chapel.

The east wall of the chapel and the beautiful early decorated window noted above is filled with trefoil and quatrefoil openings and has been assigned to Abbot de Marina (1283-86) or Hugh de Dodington (1287-94). The glass is by Hardman and illustrates the Magnificat. The side windows contain such nineteenth-century glass as survived the war and was re-set. Beneath the windows there is a fine arcade of trefoil arches with grotesque carvings in the spandrels. On the south wall is an ape represented playing pan pipes accompanied by a ram on an instrument resembling a violin with a long bow, and below is a shepherd asleep while the wolf is devouring his flock. Another shows a goat carrying a hare slung on a pole over his back, and so on. The principles underlying these carvings are difficult to interpret but the Synod of Arras in 1025 noted: 'That which the illiterate cannot apprehend from writing should be shown to them in pictures.'

On the south wall near the east window are remains of an ancient aumbry now restored to use. There are also two ancient chairs and benches. The altar arrangements are by Roland Paul.

The Elder Lady Chapel was restored and beautified by the Diocesan Mothers' Union in memory of the late Mrs Helen de Candole, wife of a Dean of Bristol, who died in February 1930. The refurnishing at that time included the lowering of the reredos and provision of a new frame for the retable, and the steps of the altar were brought back to the original medieval alignment. There are further traces of Early English work in the jambs of the large (restored) window at the north end of the north transept, and in the south transept and Newton Chapel.

In the second recess of the north choir aisle is a thirteenth-century memorial slab found in the vestibule of the chapter house. It bears an inscription including a name which, it has been suggested, may be read as William the Geometer, that is to say William the Architect.

In the fourteenth century Abbot Knowle (1306-32) undertook the major part of a scheme to rebuild the eastern section of the Abbey Church. It was planned on a much larger scale beginning some 60ft (18m) east of the Norman east wall, and its side walls were built outside the walling of the earlier work, thus enabling the old church, its sanctuary and high altar to continue in use during the course of the construction of the new work. The late Roland Paul FSA commented:

> From the dates of burials of the Berkeley family it seems clear that Knowle, after completing his Lady Chapel, first built the south aisle and the adjoining Berkeley Chapel, and afterwards the north aisle. His new north aisle incorporated the south wall of the Early English Lady Chapel - now known as the "Elder" Lady Chapel - and the consequent greater thickness of the wall at this point accounts for the deeply recessed arches, in one of which is a raised tomb, and the effigies of Lady Margaret Berkeley (1337) and her son, Maurice, Lord Berkeley (1368). Knowle was buried in front of the rood altar in the nave,

30 Aisle bridges

and his successor, Abbot Snow, was also buried there, and it is not until 1353 that we have a record of a burial in the new choir, nearly fifty years after its commencement.

Some authorities such as the late Dr John Harvey give building dates *c.*1311-40 (or after 1298) so perhaps the initial design drawings preceded Knowle. It is this fourteenth-century eastern arm of the abbey church that gives Bristol Cathedral its unique architectural quality and was the inspiration for the nineteenth-century completion of the nave.

31 Carving in Elder Lady Chapel by Adam Lock

How did the early fourteenth-century design come about, was it influenced by the height of the existing abbey, and who was the master mason designer? Marriage alliances between the English royal house and continental ones were typified by that of Henry II and Eleanor of Aquitaine, and this is a reminder of the links between Henry who spent part of his boyhood in Bristol, Angers, Poitiers and London. Poitiers, started in 1161, had Henry II and Queen Eleanor as its patrons. It was well under way in the late thirteenth century, final dedication being in 1379. Significantly perhaps it has a square east end; the general effect is however still a series of cells or compartments adding up to one space but not truly a hall-church. At Angers Cathedral a great single span vault was built and Romanesque churches with a series of virtually domed spaces were not uncommon in southern France. Another type of Romanesque church had high aisles (spatially rather separated) without clerestories.

In England, aisled retrochoirs, such as Southwark and Winchester, were developed further in the choir of the Temple Church in London (completed in 1239) to form a 'hall church', and again in the large aisled Trinity Chapel at the east end of Salisbury Cathedral (1220-25); here the designer was Elias of Derham, a friend of the family of Adam Lock. In Paris the side aisles of the lower Chapel of the Ste-Chapelle have transverse skeletal buttresses (1243-48) resembling those in the later choir aisles at Bristol. The plan of Bristol's eastern arm virtually matches the dimensions of another all but vanished Augustinian house, Merton Abbey, so it is possible that there were both London and continental links. Sir Nikolaus Pevsner also mentions St Nazaire at Carcassone. The German tradition of the Hallenkirche goes back to the Romanesque period and probably the first of the Gothic hall-churches was the nave of St. Elizabeth at Marburg (1257-83), then came Minden, Erfurt, Meissen, Olomouc, and the choir of St. Stephen's Vienna, completed in 1340.

Whatever the sources of the St. Augustine's Abbey choir, the results are spectacular. Here we have a West Country tradition (found for example at Glastonbury and in the Wells triforium) of continuous pier/arch mouldings fully realised and moulded with extraordinary refinement. This is a structurally ingenious method of transferring the main vault thrusts across the aisles to substantial external buttresses with a sacristy open vault consisting merely of ribs with no infilling, and a main lierne vault without ridge rib, but with lozenges, the cusping of which is separated from the fields (copied in the Wells choir but more timidly). Perhaps strangest of all are the stellar tomb recesses with the cusping disposed contrary to the usual practice of the time. It is worth looking into these elements more thoroughly.

Some West Country arcades before Bristol have no capitals, but it is in this Cathedral that the idea is fully worked out to achieve an exceptional upward thrust in a comparatively low interior. The inverted arches inserted under the central tower of Wells in 1338 to avert subsidence there, are similarly treated and even have the open 'eyes' that appear in a slightly different form in the Bristol choir aisle bridges. The combination of arcades (with only the smallest capitals to receive the aisle struts), a perfectly poised main vault sufficiently acute to overcome any sense of weight, large and for almost the first time elaborately transomed windows, imparts to the choir a wonderful lightness and sense of space flowing, not only east to west, but across the building as well.

In the Eastern Lady Chapel and the side aisles are recesses with cusped straight facets and inverted curved outer frames all moulded and crocketed. These half octagonal 'arches' appear in one form or another at the Bishop's Palace in St David's, Berkeley Castle, St Mary Redcliffe and a tomb in Backwell Church; in addition the much restored Lady Chapel sedilia is crowned by inverted arches calling to mind the later work at Wells.

The great north porch of St Mary Redcliffe, a mile or so away, seems to have been erected at about the same time as the Abbey choir and shares some of the odd detailing, shafts receiving vaulting without the interruption of capitals, and half octagonal setting out of entry arches. The great north door of this porch is almost the ultimate elaboration of the Cathedral wall-recess design which is perhaps related to later designs at Valladolid St Gregorio and St Pablo, and in the portal of the Capellas Imperfeitas of Batalha (1503-9) — was there a trade link here?

The sacristy of the Cathedral has curious 'skeleton' vaulting and this treatment can be found in the St David's pulpitum and the pulpitum at Southwell Minster (though there rather differently detailed). It is interesting to compare this with the choir vault of St. Mary's Warwick (1381-91) which has flying skeletal ribs, the south porch of St Vitus Cathedral Prague (*c.*1396) and the chapel of St Barbara in St. Stephen's Vienna with its hanging open ribs, which can also be found in other German examples.

The exterior of Knowle's work now appears rather severe with its embattled parapet, but it would seem from pieces of stone discovered in 1897 that an elaborate parapet was intended some 4ft 6in (1.4m) high. This parapet again was of intriguing Bristol form. All measurements were in threes: there is an equilateral triangle each side of which was trisected and from each of the two points straight lines parallel to the opposite side formed a rhombus and equilateral triangle alternating.

32 G.E. Street's sketch of proposed new nave

It is curious that when designing the nave in 1868, and thus prior to discovery of the medieval fragments, G.E. Street felt the need for open-work parapets to relieve the severity of the elevations. A further interesting feature that the master mason inserted in the Berkeley Chapel is a spherical triangular window on the lines of those in the Westminster Abbey triforium and the nave clerestory of Lichfield Cathedral. Again the striking curvilinear Great East Window has six strong vertical central lights that anticipate the Perpendicular style that was to emerge later in the fourteenth century.

The form of the fourteenth-century pulpitum (or choir screen) is not known; it may well have been on the lines of the Eastern Lady Chapel reredos or of the Tintern Abbey/Exeter 'verandah' type. In connection with Tintern, Dr Richard Morris mentions Nicholas de Durneford as a possible master mason, who may perhaps be the unknown genius at Bristol Cathedral. The late Dr Michael Smith also suggested that the architect

33 G.E. Street's proposed west front of cathedral

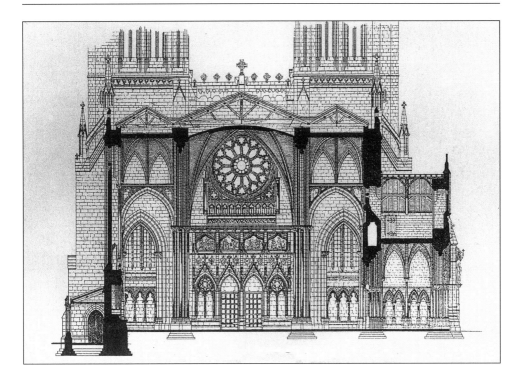

34 G.E. Street's proposed new nave, transverse section

for the choir might be Nicholas de Durneford, adding that 'his hand may be recognisable at Beaumaris, where he is recorded in Royal Service, at St Mark's (the Lord Mayor's Chapel), and perhaps at Clevedon' (Court).

The main mid-fourteenth century work at Redcliffe is closely allied to that at Wells by William Joy, and the physiognomy from then on is very different from that of St Augustine's Abbey. Indeed, Redcliffe in rebuilding the Early English church was, save for the north porch and stellar tomb recesses, uninfluenced by its neighbour.

Once the choir was finished, completion of the Newton Chapel, the vaulting of the transepts, and insertion of more up-to-date windows in them, appear to have been the only structural changes until the rebuilding of the Norman central tower was undertaken. The central tower rises to a height of some 136ft and is of considerable girth, but the full height aisles of nave and choir tend to reduce its impact when seen at close quarters. The noble and restrained design consists of two stages of five main blind and traceried lights, three sets of twin upper lights, on each face being louvred to emit bell sound. A Bristol and North Somerset feature is the emphasised north-east angle vice, or stair turret, surmounted by a larger pinnacle than those on the other three corners of the tower. The parapets are battlemented and carved with an arcade; the whole design seems to be related to the earlier Hereford Cathedral central tower and the multiple-windowed Midland church towers such as St Mary Nottingham, Melton Mowbray, Coleshill, Loughborough and Kings Norton.

35 Cathedral in fifteenth century

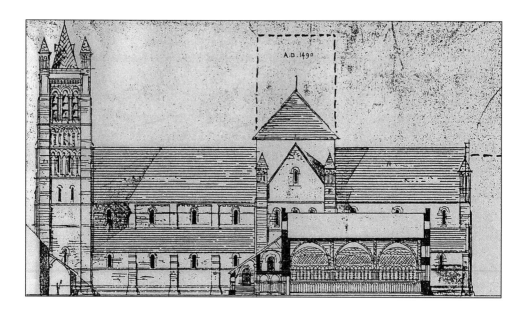

36 South elevation of the cathedral

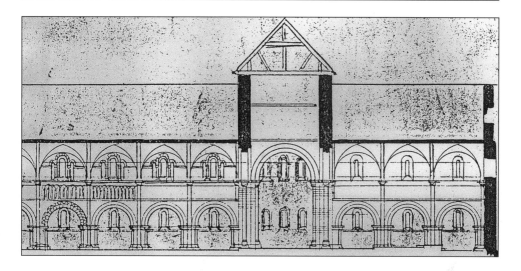

37 Section looking north

The Commissioners of King Edward VI (1533) recorded a medieval ring of nine or ten bells within the tower, of which four remain in the great medieval frame. The surviving chiming bells are of considerable interest and date from circa 1300, 1480, 1500 and a bell recast in 1670. The Reverend David Cawley notes that:

> The ancient third bell must have hung in the previous (Norman) tower of the Cathedral; the treble and second bells although of approximately of the same age and from the Bristol foundry differ in ornament and are from different hands. The treble is of interest as it bears both the pierced head rebus and the initials I N of Abbot John Newland ("Nailheart") 1481-1515. The second is a most rare example and only three other bells are known by this founder. The tenor bell is, as stated, probably a recasting of a slightly heavier and deeper toned medieval bell; the present one is by Roger Purdue II and was cast in Bristol in 1670.

Returning now to the interior, it is noticeable that the south transept vault lacks the vitality and clarity of the earlier work; indeed two main and hidden transverse structural ribs appear as a ridge in the vault fields. The North transept vault is better handled and bears some very fine bosses. The Newton Chapel attached to the south aisle probably dates from the time of Abbots Snow and Ashe (1332-52) and contains the tombs of members of the Newton family of Bowers Court in Kingswood. The chapel probably stands on the site of a Norman apsidal one. Architecturally it is not as stirring as the rest of the choir but it is an interesting example of late Decorated, bordering on Perpendicular, when the motifs seen in the earlier parts of the building ceased to be used. The east window contains good tracery and glass. The shortened arches in the south and west walls are probably due to the rebuilding of the transept by Abbot Newland in 1481-1515, and

38 Skeleton vault

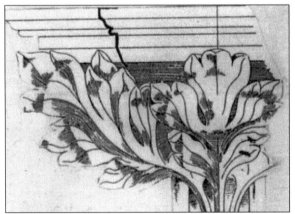

39 Canopied niche

40 Natural forms

*41 Carving Elder Lady
Chapel. St Michael*

*42 Animals playing
musical instruments*

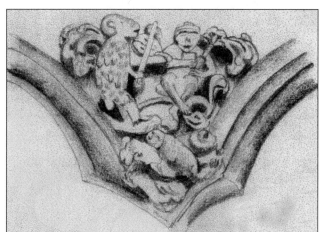

43 Goat playing a horn

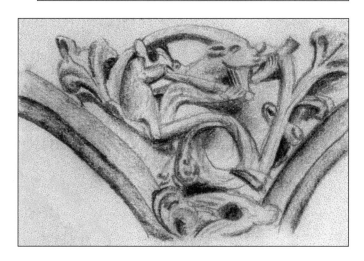

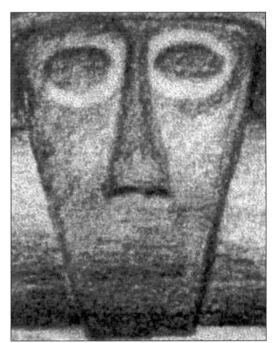

44-49   Carved heads

the west arch contains a good piece of typical Bristol Tudor screenwork. The panelled altar tomb against the east wall, with a flat decorated canopy, is of the type known as a chantry tomb, having an opening at one end to be used by the priest when he chanted the Masses for the repose of the dead. According to the inscription it is the tomb of Sir Richard Newton Craddock who died in 1448. It is not clear whether this tomb has been moved from its original position; normally it would have been against a south wall so that the priest could face east. This south wall is now, however, occupied by a massive altar tomb to Sir Henry Newton (1599) and Catherine, his wife, with their six children in relief on the front surface.

There is yet another tomb in this small chapel, this time with twisted pillars and a lofty canopy, which has an armoured effigy of Sir John Newton Bart (died 1661) holding a truncheon in his right hand. Sir John had taken part in the Civil War and was 'a man of great courage and the greatest loyalty to his Prince and honour to his Country'. Squeezed between these two monuments, in the south wall, there is an early English piscina. There are other monuments in the chapel: to Charlotte Stanhope (by Westmacott), to the children of Dean Lamb and to Bishop Jonathan Trelawny. The Newton Chapel was restored and refurnished in November 1931 with an altar, throw-over frontal and ancient benches and rich carpet, in memory of the late Canon Edward Pattison Cole and his wife. The shields on the fine Comper-like wrought iron screen bear the arms of the Cathedral, the Dean, the Bishop of the City, and the Cole and Newton families. Unfortunately this refurnishing has now been dispersed.

The monastic sacristy is now the vestibule of the Berkeley Chapel and is thought to be the work of Abbot Knowle (1306-32). On the aisle side it has a fine Decorated doorway with blank recesses and high pinnacle buttresses on each side, all much restored. The finials of the gables are elaborately carved representations of the pomegranate. The Arms of the Berkeleys are displayed above the doorway. Facing the entrance are three ogee arches of uncommon design, with niches between them. All this work is extremely naturalistic and beautifully carved. One of the arches has a hearth which may have been used for baking the sacramental wafer or heating the coals for the service of the censer, and the flue above it has an outlet in a pinnacle of the Berkeley Chapel. Reference has already been made to the remarkable vaulted roof of the sacristy, but even the doorway leading into the Berkeley Chapel itself is rather an oddity. It has crockets — often described as representing ammonites, but now held to be the fruit of the medicago, or medick, which is coiled into a spiral — and below is a moulding of medlars.

The Berkeley Chapel itself was dedicated originally to the Virgin Mary, and its present name comes from Thomas, Lord of Berkeley, who died in 1348, and who founded a chantry for the soul of his wife Margaret who died in 1337. There are two piscinae and raised altar steps beneath the east windows, together with two excellent stone reredoses by Roland Paul. The twin altars were probably originally separated by a screen; there is a tradition that one of the altars was dedicated to St Keyna, who occupied a hermitage at Keynsham and is supposed to have turned the snakes in the district into stone.

There are large ballflowers in the window recesses and soffits. Again, the aumbries in the south wall are of a most curious design and the north wall of the chapel is pierced by a stellar arch, beneath which is carving of a much earlier date (thirteenth century) inserted as a feature.

This chapel was restored and refurnished in 1924-5 by Captain Mardon as a memorial to his wife, and was set apart for the use of boys and girls of the city. A stained glass window over the boys' altar represents St Christopher, and the window over the girls' altar St Anne instructing the Blessed Virgin. The south window depicts scenes from the childhood of Christ. This excellent glass is by Arnold Robinson, a pupil of Christopher Whall.

The branched chandelier in the Berkeley Chapel is made of latten and was rescued from the Temple Church when this was burnt out during the War. At the top of the chandelier is a statuette of the Madonna and Child and within the Tabernacle are St George and the Dragon. The chandelier is not entirely unique but is one of about a dozen similar ones, imported like the eagle lectern in St Stephen's City, from Flanders.

At the east end of the nave of nearly every medieval cathedral and monastic church stood the pulpitum or choir screen, before which there was often a separate rood screen. At Bristol there are references to Abbots' burials; 'under a brode marbull stone.... before the Rode Auter' is a typical description. The pulpitum was sited where the present screen is, and there was a rood screen between the western piers of the central tower. No trace of the original pulpitum, with a 'dore going to the loft going to the organs', remains.

The choir stalls of 1512-26 have incorporated an enormous amount of interesting carving, with heraldic devices and the arms of Abbot Elyot, with the initials R.E. and the Berkeley family supported by mermaids and surmounted by a mitre. The original woodwork panel frames and the fronts of the canons' stalls contain wonderful designs with birds and grotesque animals in the spandrels; the cresting above the stalls is also largely original. The misericords are of particularly good design and contain much spirited carving: the subjects include incidents from the popular medieval tale of Reynard the Fox, the representation of medieval sports and pastimes, and scenes from rural and domestic life. Three were considered improper and removed from the Cathedral in the nineteenth century.

The Norman nave seems to have become ruinous and the replacement nave intended by Abbot Newland had apparently only reached cill height, so the newly-established Cathedral lacked a screen for sub-division of the truncated interior. A merchant, Thomas White, left the stone screen of the White Friars or Carmelite church (seized in 1539) in his will to the newly constituted Cathedral: 'I give and bequethe unto my Cathedral church, called the Trynyte of Bristol the Quere which was sometime in the White ffriers … to be sett upp at my cost and charge'. No trace remains of the elaborately-panelled central doorway (on the lines of one in Bristol Museum), but the side sections and carving, consigned in 1860 to a dump in the churchyard, were rebuilt by J.L. Pearson into the flanking walls of the sedilia. The Royal Arms of Henry VIII, with the dragon and greyhound as supporters, and the arms of Prince Edward supported by beautiful scrolls of roses and leaves beneath the initials P.E. are also to be seen on the White Friars Screen as re-erected.

On the demolition of the nave a re-arrangement of the interior was essential for continued worship. In 1542 the monastic internal arrangements were greatly altered including removal of the great pulpitum, rood screen and high altar. A new high altar was erected in front of the fourteenth-century reredos in the Eastern Lady Chapel and the White Friars Screen was erected to create a nave or ante-chapel. The truncated nave was eventually provided with a fine pulpit and pews. The medieval parclose screens were re-set at mid-length in the choir aisles. Upon the White Friars Screen, which formed the sub-division, stood the great organ by Renatus Harris. This was corbelled out because of the comparative narrowness of the screen below, and there was a loft running the full width of the screen. The west side of the White Friars Screen seems originally to have had statues, because in 1561 the Queen's Commissioners ordered that the 'divers tabernacles for images in the fronture of the Roodloft … be defaced and hewn down and afterward to be made a playne wall'. However, flat paintings of the minor prophets seem to have taken the place of the statues and these in turn were expunged during the Commonwealth. In 1557 the Privy Council admonished the mayor and aldermen 'not to absent themselves' or wait for the dean and chapter to 'fetch them out of the city with their cross and procession, being the same is very unseemly'. So by 1606 a gallery was constructed near the nave pulpit by the corporation (with chapter permission). But this gallery was eventually erected only 3ft off the ground because the Bishop objected; he said a higher erection made the cathedral look like a playhouse. The bishop also moved the pulpit almost out of earshot, so the corporation then departed to St Mary Redcliffe for sermons!

The newly constituted Cathedral now endured the vicissitudes typical of the times. Gerald Cobb notes that in 1634 three tourists from Norwich came to Bristol and reported that 'in the cathedral are rich organs, lately beautified; and indifferent good Quiresters'. But this was all to change. The organ was destroyed in the Civil War (Bristol had its fair share of iconoclastic puritans) and the lead roof of the Bishop's Palace, which stood to the south east of the churchyard, was stripped off while Bishop Howell was in residence and his wife in labour. She died from exposure and the Bishop and his family of eight children were thrown out. One Walter Deyor had lead removed from the roofs of the Cathedral and cloisters but fortunately was prevented from carrying out further damage by some members of the Corporation. The Palace even became a brewery for some years!

After the Restoration of King Charles II there was a gradual return to decency. Indeed, in the eighteenth century Browne Willis reports that the 'interior is so well adorned that it wants for no cost or art to render it beautiful, and is daily improving and may be said to be kept in as good repair as any church whatsoever'. The splendid organ cases of 1683 remain to this day, no longer centrally on a pulpitum but side by side on the north side of the choir. When the organ cases stood upon the pulpitum they were surmounted by great finials topped with mitres and crowns (two of which remain bracketed from the north side of the present aisle case). There was also a smaller and beautiful choir or ruckpositive case on the east side in the usual position over the entrance to the choir.

By the 1860s the organ had been moved to the north side of the choir, the finials lopped off and the positive case replaced by a typical nineteenth-century one of the dullest, incorrect, and unsympathetic design. This in its turn disappeared when the organ and choir stalls were moved westward to their present site.

Today the Eastern Lady Chapel reredos is surmounted by a later medieval cresting and openwork parapet. There is uncertainty as to the central opening of the three-arched design. There are references to the gilding and repair of the classical reredos, shown in a pre-1839 drawing, and an attribution to an Inigo Jones design posthumously executed. Apparently when this reredos was removed the central section of the medieval work was found to be defaced, although it was shown complete in Hacker's drawing of 1828.

During these upheavals the Cathedral comprised the eastern arm and chapels complete, the central tower supported to the west by the responds of Newland's projected nave, and with a window of 1629 in the blocking west wall. The remains of the monastery were built into houses; indeed dwellings were erected on the site of the nave and these remained until 1835.

The cloister and monastic buildings were to the south of the abbey church on a falling site. The night stair from the church to the rere-dorter exists, but the dorter sub vault, divided into two aisles with two or three columns in the centre and some 29ft (9m) wide, was eventually replaced in 1923 by fine vestries, slype passage and song school by Roland Paul FSA. There is a beautiful thirteenth-century doorway leading from the now vanished west cloister walk into the School.

The plague of 1349 and extensive work to the church prevented much work being carried out to the monastic building. However, Newland's Chronicle reports the earlier erection by Abbot Knowle of the King's Hall and King's Chamber and that he 'repaired and covered the Frater'. The only fourteenth-century work now existing is in the ex-Deanery part of the School. At this time the cloister court was enlarged by about 10ft, and some walling remains at low level.

Abbot Newland, who was appointed in 1481, carried out considerable work to the monastic buildings, including the Prior's Lodging, the great gatehouse in the outer court, the almonry, hay barn and the stables. Subsequently there have been countless modifications and demolitions, including the Minster House south-west of the nave and the Old Deanery which stood to the west of and was attached to the west of the great gate.

The lesser cloister plan is still discernible, south of the frater (Cathedral school).

Despite the post-Dissolution and Reformation vicissitudes, major parts of the monastic buildings survived. These include the frater or refectory, now sub-divided and part of the Cathedral School; the chapter house and vestibule; the east and north walks of the cloister, the latter somewhat mutilated and later to be reconstructed by Street; the rere-dorter passage; the Norman sub-croft; and on the site of the cellarium, the Abbot's Lodge, to the west of the cloister various converted houses such as the now vanished Minster House. The great gatehouse to the outer court also survived as it does to this day. To the south-east was the Bishop's Palace, the remains of which were sadly not recorded and not even well photographed prior to demolition in the 1960s. The fenestration of the frater points to very late Perpendicular re-modelling and this in its turn was in part refaced, probably by R.S. or T.S. Pope fairly early in the nineteenth century.

By the 1850s the condition of the central tower, which was very inadequately buttressed on the west side, was giving concern and the great engineer Isambard Brunel was consulted. The Dean of the day, Gilbert Elliott, invited him to examine defects in the Cathedral fabric. On June 1 1850, Brunel responded and wrote that he proposed to 'give a couple of hours for a cursory inspection to form some opinion of the subject'. It was brief because he continued: 'I can be at the Cathedral at 5 o'clock on Tuesday morning next, having to leave Bristol by train to Exeter at 7.50'. An early start indeed!

On June 24 he wrote to the Dean to report upon his examination. He refers favourably to the work of a Mr Welsh but differs from him in thinking that the troubles are those of any old building and present no immediate threat. Brunel wrote: 'Mr Welsh no doubt would feel little anxiety at the building standing 24 hours — I feel little as to its standing 24 years — we both feel that repairs are required.... The next or the following generation will probably be called upon for more extensive repairs and restoration.' Thereafter Brunel disappears from the Cathedral scene. There was a restoration programme but he had no part in it; as he wrote, correctly, there was need for an architect to do the work.

Moves to carry out repairs and to rebuild the nave were prompted by the condition of the tower and by suggestions in *The Ecclesiologist* that rather than re-order it would be better to raise funds for reconstruction, since there is a need for more congregational accommodation in the Cathedral of a great and thriving city.

The T.S. Pope stone and marble choir screen of 1860, which was not joined to the stalls still in their previous position, did not last long. This was probably just as well. *The Ecclesiologist* had described it as looking like 'a gate to a field with the hedges taken away'.

In December 1866 the building committee appointed George Edmund Street (1824-81) as its architect. Street had intended to take Orders but having changed his mind joined the office of Scott & Moffat, later to be dominated by the surviving partner Sir Gilbert Scott. Scott had given some general advice prior to the disastrous re-ordering carried out by T S Pope in 1860-61, but Bristol was one of only a dozen cathedrals where he carried out no work.

Street was a member of the Ecclesiological Society, was Diocesan architect for Oxford, was on the Council of the English Church Union and was for a time Churchwarden of All Saints, St. Margaret Street. He was responsible for innumerable churches such as All Saints Clifton, and restorations such as that of Christchurch Cathedral, Dublin. He and

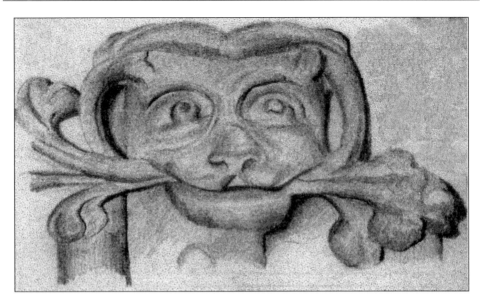

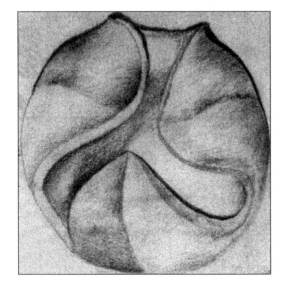

from top:
50 *Monkey carving*
51 *South wall niches*
52 *Carving*

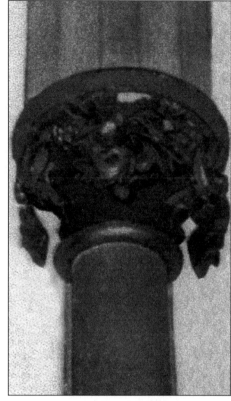

53 & 54 Carvings

the moving spirit for completion, Canon Norris, would have had much in common but, as the later statue controversy proved, Street and the evangelical Dean were, one assumes, not so close.

In 1866 Street was one of the ten architects originally invited to compete for the design of a new National Gallery and one of six for the new Courts of Law. Street came second in the Law Courts commission but was finally awarded the design. He suffered an enormous volume of ignorant and noisy criticism, maddening official vacillation and cheese-paring, and all the usual troubles associated with a major building project of this sort. The vast variety of detail in all these buildings, including the nave at Bristol is the product of one mind, and in the end the work killed him. As Goodhart Rendell noted,:

> 'in the fifteen years before his death in 1881, Street, who had learnt the answers to everything in the line of work he had mapped out for himself, had nothing to do but produce and produce, as long as his health would stand it. Until his last year on earth he had never had a headache or a toothache and the two paralytic strokes that quickly ended his life at the age of 57 were preceded by no incapacitation.'

The task of completing a cathedral, the choir of which was a work of unique originality and genius, could hardly have been more difficult. There had, of course, been earlier proposals in the 1840s and '50s to build a nave on the site of the vanished Norman nave of the Cathedral and the projected medieval work, which had only reached the cills of the windows. In 1840 T. Willson prepared a design with twin octagonal towers at the west end and a balancing Elder Lady Chapel west of the north transept. The choice of Street to build the new nave was an inspired one, as he was a formidably original yet sympathetic architect. The mandate was to build a nave such as Abbot Knowle would have built had he lived. Street said that he wished to build a nave in harmony with Knowle's choir, but with such a freedom in treatment as would show no mere slavish imitation of the earlier model. He wrote the following on the matter: 'I should wish to mark by a few minor alterations such as the sections of the mouldings, the designs of the window traceries, and the character of the sculpture, the fact that this new nave is really the work of the nineteenth century not of the fourteenth.'

Street's earlier churches tend to 'have an excess and boldness or bluntness, a tinge of eccentricity, a truthfulness in displaying construction, which is too much like that of a candid friend. But if excuse is wanted it will be found in the intention with which such work was done. It was the strongest form of protest against that dull and meaningless symmetry which had long been the leading character of church architecture before the revival. And if my father laid himself open to the charge of exaggeration he did so in good company.' So wrote his son A.E .Street. This forthright approach was just what was needed to complete work by an earlier exponent of boldness and originality.

A report in *The Builder* in 1868 very clearly describes Street's intentions and the basis of his thinking:

> In 1866 considerable alterations were made in the road at the north side of the cathedral, access on this side being improved by the removal of the earth to a depth of several feet. The excavations thus made laid open to view the foundations of a nave and north porch. Previously to these discoveries, a movement had already been set on foot for the completion of the cathedral by the erection of a nave. The public attention drawn to the discovery gave an impetus to the efforts of Canon Norris and his friends, and the private subscriptions increased; and on the appointment of Mr G.E. Street as architect he submitted plans for the building of the nave with western frontage and steeples or towers. His report was considered at a public meeting in June 1867. The general design of his plan was to copy very closely the work in the present choir, with a few minor alterations, such as the sections of mouldings, the design of the window tracery, and the character of the sculpture, sufficiently to show that the new nave was really a work of the nineteenth century and not of the fourteenth. He believed, however, that this would be in such complete harmony with the old work that in the general *coup d'oeil* no difference would be noticed between the two works. With regard to the western front, he believed that the old plan did not contemplate steeples, but in his opinion the cathedral would in all respects be a more striking and effective building if it were finished with two western steeples than if it had simply a nave and aisles corresponding with and very nearly repeating the outline of the existing eastern

55 Scott's screen of 1860

portion of the church. The addition of the nave and western steeples would give the whole a bulk and importance which would make the cathedral — as it ought to be — the most conspicuous object in the distant view of the city; and it would then have so unmistakeably the character of the cathedral church that every one would be at once impressed with its appearance. The plan was adopted. The cost of the whole work was estimated at upwards of £50,000, and having obtained promises amounting to upwards of £15,000, the committee felt themselves in a position to commence work so early as October or November last. The whole nave will have a length of 117 feet from the transept tower, and a width of about 80 ft. It will be furnished with north and south-western towers 130 ft high, and have a northern and western frontage, and connected with it on the southern side will be the original cloisters, the architect having introduced an arcading or arched corridor in this part of his plan. The nave will be built of Doulting stone.

Street cleverly altered the side aisle vaults to a sexpartite form and similarly the wall recesses, which would have been so easy to copy from the medieval work, were 'normalised'. This was an act of self-abnegation, not always appreciated by some critics who mistakenly feel that Street was trying to improve on the earlier work. He fully appreciated it as it stood and indeed was so taken with the medieval Master's work that he repeated a Bristol strainer arch at the west end of St Peter's Bournemouth. The west front too has had its critics, but adding such a front to a cathedral with aisles and nave of equal height poses considerable problems of proportion.

After Street's sudden death in 1881 the towers were completed by another very great architect, John Loughborough Pearson, surveyor of Westminster Abbey and the designer of Truro Cathedral, St Stephen's Bournemouth, and many other fine churches. It is to Pearson that we owe the superb sanctuary furnishings, reredos, pavement and so on. And it was Pearson who decided not to adopt Street's hipped roofs on the west tower which, although they might have met objections to the nearly equal height of the three towers, were not perhaps an entirely happy inspiration.

Within the north-west tower is a fine ring of eight bells formerly hung in the tower of the Temple Church. The bells, in the key of E flat, are listed in the table (right).

The Pearson work, completed after his death by his son Frank, could hardly be bettered. The high altar reredos stands on the site of the original medieval high altar, which was marked by a change in the vault elaboration.

The reredos is filled with figures of biblical saints, bishops connected with the See of Bristol, and local celebrities including William Canynges and Hannah More. The general idea of the central portion illustrates the Te Deum — the glorious company of the apostles, the goodly fellowship of the prophets, the noble army of martyrs, and the holy church throughout the world. It was erected in 1899 from designs by Pearson at a cost of £2500 to commemorate Bishop Ellicott's long association with the Diocese of Bristol and Gloucester, and it occupies the original position of the high altar of Abbot Knowle's choir. The side sections which separate the eastern bay of the choir from the Eastern Lady Chapel, and flank the reredos on each side, contain figures of saints to whom local

Bell	Diameter	Note	Weight	Date	Founder
Tenor	4'1"	*309cps	21-0-1	1887	John Taylor & Co. Loughborough
7th	3'7½"		13-3-12	"	"
6th	3'3¼"		10-3-10	"	"
5th	3'2⅜"		10-1-0	"	"
4th	3'0¼"		8-1-24	1740	Thos. Bilbie, Chewstowe
3rd	2'10⅜"		8-3-24	1658	Wm. & Roger Purdue, Bristol
2nd	2'9¼"		8-1-8	1726	Thos. Bilbie
Treble	2'9⅜"		8-2-8	1726	Thos. Bilbie

Above   The eight bells of the north-west tower

churches are dedicated.

The reredos is superbly detailed, as is the great cosmati-type pavement, and with that at Peterborough Cathedral is arguably one of his finest. The two sedilia cleverly incorporate on the aisle side the remains of the White Friars screens. Also felicitously detailed is the adjoining ironwork, and the fine brass altar rails. As part of the same restoration, Pearson also sympathetically repaired the late medieval choir stalls with their splendid misericords, and elaborate traceried stall ends and canopies.

Then came the fine stone open choir screen. This properly subdivides the Cathedral without obstructing its use on occasion as one building. Those cathedrals where screens have been mistakenly removed lose mystery, apparent length, scale, and the subdivision essential to a great church always intended by their original designers. The choir screen was erected in 1905 as a memorial to the late W. Killigrew Wait, from designs by J.L. Pearson, carried out by his son Frank. The niches contain figures of notable persons connected with the history of the Cathedral and saints of the English church. The choir screen is of three bays with two smaller canted ones and seems to have been inspired by that at Lierre near Antwerp; it is, however, typically Pearson in all its detail.

Thereafter the next Cathedral architect and antiquary Roland Paul carried out much furnishing work, the Eastern Lady Chapel side parapets, the choir pulpit (with its ancient traceried panels), the Berkeley Chapel reredoses and kneelers, the Elder Lady Chapel altar, the Bishop's throne and the choir vestries of 1923. Subsequently the iron screen to the Newton Chapel and its now dispersed furnishings, plus the High Altar standard candlesticks and those around Street's font in the baptistery were added to the design, perhaps by Randoll Blacking. Through the late 1930s till his death in May 1950, Sir

George Oatley, the designer of the great tower of the University, was Cathedral architect, and to him we owe the inner lobby of the north porch, the glazing of the west doors and nave sanctuary kneelers. It was during the same period that Professor Tristram conserved and enhanced the polychrome of the Eastern Lady Chapel and the bosses of the choir, the nave also being enlivened with some restrained gilding and colour.

6 The monuments of the cathedral

Since the Abbey-Cathedral was bereft of a nave for about 400 years, the monuments which form a significant part of the heritage of the Cathedral are to be found mainly east of the transepts, and to a lesser extent within. However, all the main types of funerary monuments can be found within the building.

The earliest style of memorial was a simple grave slab cut out of stone, which was introduced into the floor of the church. This was one-dimensional art, but in the twelfth century it gave way to something more approaching a three-dimensional format. Recumbent figures are seen in the round. A third stage is reached when the tomb is constructed in the form of a large chest. This becomes further refined with quatrefoil canopies and with the addition of heraldic symbols. From the sixteenth century onwards, the influence of the Renaissance begins to be felt with the introduction of balusters and pilasters, and a general imitation of what might be called the Roman Imperial Style. However, this was not always carried off with an appropriate sense of classical proportion, and the effect is sometimes both awkward and stiff.

The Baroque style followed where the monuments have a dramatic character and aim, clearly, to impress the viewer. The memory of the departed is asserted with some éclat. Marble is often used instead of local stone, supposedly in keeping with the classical tradition. The effigies are often held within a carefully-defined frame and the total effect is not unlike that of a reredos, with the dead person commemorated instead of the figure on the cross.

The later eighteenth century saw a return to a more Grecian classicism. The portrayal of drapery in stone becomes common. Colour, however, does not appear to have been used, even though it was a conspicuous feature of Greco-Roman art. Men appear sometimes in classical garb, as do the women; the influence of the statuary of Athens is clearly influential. There is often a plain rectangular frame with a shallow pediment and at the bottom, contained within this frame, a figure is placed in high relief. The naturalism for which the Romantic movement stood is evident in this portrayal of the figures. All this gave way before the force of the Gothic Revival ushered in by the Romantic Movement. The nineteenth century discovered what it called the Middle Ages, and medievalism entered into the language. Funerary monuments were once more erected in the forms of chests, with their canopies and other characteristic features. Bishops, deans and canons lay in the same recumbent posture as the knights and clerics of old. Sometimes the memorials are overwhelming in their fussiness. There appears to be a sheer delight not only in what has been rediscovered but also in the modern technology that made such work both more elaborate and easier to execute than was ever possible during medieval times. This Gothic style lingered on into the twentieth century, at least until after the 1914-18 war. After that something more sober came to the fore. The memorials to the fallen appear to be the last expression of the genre; thereafter there is a greater simplicity, even austerity: name, dates, appointments and, if necessary, heraldic symbols suffice.

These various stages are visible in the Cathedral. The earliest type lies at the entrance to the Elder Lady Chapel and is the gravestone of Abbot David, the abbot under whose rule the chapel was built. The date is likely to be soon after 1253, the year in which he died. The right arm of the cross is decipherable and there is a simple border. It may be that there is also the portrayal of a man with curly hair. On the whole, even though much worn by time, this seems to be a wholly appropriate memorial for a canon whose order was noted for its modesty. A stone of a similar kind is to be found at Almondsbury where the abbey had an estate that was also a favourite retreat for the abbots.

The second stage of development can be studied in the funerary memorials to Maurice and Thomas Berkeley, which lie in the south choir aisle, and of the abbots in the Eastern Lady Chapel. Here the portrayal of the canons and warrior knights is more dramatic. The cross-legged knight is thought to be Thomas, sixth Lord Berkeley (d.1321) and the straight-legged one is considered to be Maurice III, seventh Lord Berkeley (d.1326). We need not think that these were life-like effigies. Often these memorials were intended to be symbolic rather than realistic. They may even have been ordered and executed before the death of the person commemorated. On the other hand they may have been produced long after the death of the person remembered. There is no means of knowing since there is little firm evidence on which dating of the work can be based. The generalities of style are the determinants.

On the north side of the Berkeley Chapel there is a solid chest tomb, which is important even though it has been treated badly over the years. Beneath a massive Early English slab there is a heraldic panel which records the marriage of Thomas Berkeley to his second wife Joan Quincey who died on March 19 1309, after having been married for 42 years; no small achievement at a time of relatively short life expectancy. This is thought to be her burial place and that her image is here.

Maurice's monument between the Elder Lady Chapel and the north choir aisle is well preserved. The chain mail which was once executed in gesso has been smoothed out. Over this mail is shown a quilted haketon, a hauberk and surcoat held in place by a narrow belt. The sword is huge: the same size as the sword by the side of the coronation chair in Westminster Abbey. Thomas's shield has the Berkeley arms carved upon it and is supported by a broad strap. On the knees are poleyns, probably in real life made of leather and a step on the way towards the development of plate armour. The feet of the knight have pryck spurs and the feet rest upon the traditional lion. His head rests upon two cushions set diagonally and supported by a pair of angels. This design had been used before at the tomb of Edmund Crouchback, Earl of Lancaster (d.1296). The lady too has her head resting upon a pair of cushions, also supported by angels. She is dressed in a style that indicates the monument can be dated to the early years of the fourteenth century.

Thomas Berkeley was a soldier who had fought with Prince Edward. He was present at the Battle of Evesham where Simon de Montfort was killed. Later he served Edward II and was present at the Battle of Bannockburn (June 24 1314). During that disastrous

English defeat he was captured, but was ransomed the next year, no doubt at some cost to the family estates.

The monument to Maurice IV is in the south recess of the Elder Lady Chapel. Here he lies in a very substantial tomb chest alongside his mother, Margaret, who was the first wife of Thomas. His shoulders, arms and legs are protected by quilted plate, perhaps originally made of leather and riveted on to metal splints. The gauntlets, knee belts and short dagger are all reasonably well preserved. There is no shield: instead the Berkeley arms are carried upon the jupon. The Berkeley crest is on the top of the helmet on which his head rests. These monuments would, of course, have been finished in full colour, rather like the tombs of the abbots in the Eastern Lady Chapel. Now, in the modern fashion for conservation, they all lie in their grey stone colour.

The Berkeley tombs are arranged as follows:

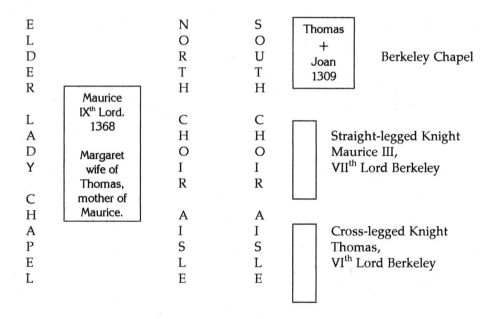

Something of the colour used on medieval monuments can be seen on the tombs of the abbots, who lie in the Eastern Lady Chapel: Abbots Hunt and Newbury on the north side and Abbot Newland on the south. The design here, and elsewhere in the medieval part of the Cathedral, is idiosyncratic. There is a cusped recess in each case of a semi-octagonal shape, surrounded by a design resembling a star. This effect is achieved by placing a number of arcs convex-wise around the recess, with a leaf-like finial wherever two arcs meet. They have been restored, as part of the programme to restore the Eastern Lady Chapel to its presumed original coloration. They stand in strong contrast with the greyness of the unrestored Berkeley knights. Prints from earlier times suggest that these monuments had not been degraded either at the Reformation or during the Commonwealth. The restoration work on the tombs of the abbots would then appear to have been carried out conservatively. These memorials constitute one of the relatively few places where such undamaged monuments can be seen. The faces seem to be real and symbolic, and the carving and stonework are clean, pure and vital.

The monument to Paul Bush, the first Bishop of Bristol, shows a development from the solid tomb chest. Now the monument is opened up in the form of a two-storey tomb. The bishop is not commemorated in all his glory but as a semi-decomposed cadaver. Often such two-level tombs also presented the deceased as he was in life, generally in his robes of office. This is not the case here: the emphasis is upon mortality. There is a certain preoccupation with death, which in some ways became a major theme during this period. Since Bush had been a student of medicine at Oxford it may be that the design of the tomb was intended to allude to this earlier concern. He came to Bristol after being Prior to the Community at the Church of the Bonhommes, at Edington in Wiltshire. Old monks reappeared with secular order responsibilities. Later he married and, though he was a widower by the time that Mary reviewed him in her counter-Reformation, he was removed and spent his time in the benefice of Winterbourne where he was also the rector.

Gradually the influence of the Renaissance makes its influence felt, as may be seen from the monuments in the Newton Chapel. The figures are stiff and seem awkward, but if attention is paid to the surrounding decoration the classical allusion seems clear enough. Two other monuments in the same general style are to be found at the west end of the Cathedral. For these it is sufficient to note that they were originally placed elsewhere, and only took their present positions after the nave was completed towards the end of the nineteenth century. While there may seem to be a certain absence of fluidity of line in the figures, it may be that the postures are intended to convey an attitude of deep thought or devotion. Further, male armour and female attire were indeed stiff.

Freer movement comes in with the Baroque and Rococo idioms of the eighteenth century. There figures appear in high relief, sometimes contained within a medallion. This is clearly the case with the Daniel monument in the north cloister and the Gore memorial in the north transept. The Grecian aspect of funerary monuments to which reference was made earlier now comes to the fore through the work of James Stuart (1713-88). He was both a painter and an architect who had studied in Rome, Italy and above all in Athens. His publication of the antiquities there in 1762 had a profound effect, so much so that this Grecian classical style became widely adopted. The Mason memorial is his. The emphasis upon a flowing line, geometric shape and naturalism is well shown in the Middleton memorial located in the south choir aisle. A woman kneels in an attitude of devotion at the side of a severe stele. The portrayal of the clothing in marble is realistic, striking and graceful. The monument was executed by Edward Baily (1788-1867), a Bristolian who became a pupil of Flaxman after a false start as the carver of figure heads for ships. His statue for the Bristol Literary Institute made his reputation. For most of his career he devoted himself to the production of statues and busts with a mainly domestic, rather than a classical, emphasis. His studies of Charles James Fox and Lord Mansfield adorn St Stephen's Hall, Westminster. Graceful as this monument is, it is not unique, for an identical one is to be found in Buckden Church, Cambridgeshire. Evidently he had his design and pattern books. This is only to be expected: it was, after all, the practice in the Roman Empire. Figures were mass-produced and the details of the head and face were added later as required. Baily was also responsible for the bust of Robert Southey that stands in the north choir aisle. Again the emphasis is upon visual realism.

John Bacon (1740-99) may have had little sympathy for classical art but he was, nonetheless, affected by it as his monuments show. Like Baily, he had enjoyed a brilliant time at the Academy. He was well known for his statues of William Pitt at the Guildhall, Johnson and Howard at St Paul's, Blackstone at All Souls, and perhaps above all for his gigantic statue of King George III outside Somerset House. He also executed the statue of Thomas Gray that stands in Westminster Abbey.

The memorial to Elizabeth Draper, generally known as Eliza, consists of two women mourning on either side of an urn set on a pedestal. The inscription makes clear that the two figures are Genius with a torch, and Benevolence holding a pelican feeding her young. Bacon was to use this symbol of the pelican with some frequency in his work, as well as the figure of the mourning woman. His monument is the finest for its period to be found in the Cathedral.

Eliza herself connects Bristol with a wider and different world. Her father had worked for the East India Company and she was born at Anjengo on the Malabar coast on April 5 1744. After the death of her parents she returned to England for a short time between 1754 and 1757, when she returned once more to India and married Daniel Draper, Secretary to the Governor of Bombay. He was 32, she was 14. At the age of 22 she returned to England again where, in January 1767, she met the novelist Laurence Sterne at a house in London. Obviously there was some instant rapport, for when she returned to Bombay the following April she and Sterne had agreed to keep journals. Part of his journal has survived and shows the extent to which he kept her in mind. When he published *The Sentimental Journey* in 1768 the extent of his remembrance became clear. Eliza remained in India until January 11 1773 when she left her husband, escaping from him and the house by means of a rope. This caused a sensation and gave her notoriety. This she also acquired in England after the posthumous publication of *Letters from Yorick to Eliza*. She left London for an unknown reason in 1775 to settle in Clifton, where she died on August 3 1778. She left no literary remains.

The Cathedral also contains other sculptures by distinguished artists. The memorial to Emma Crauford was wrought by Sir Charles Chantrey (1781-1841). He produced many busts including those for George III, and of the Admirals for the College at Greenwich. J. Havard Thomas (1813-62) executed the memorial to Mary Carpenter, and was also responsible for sculptural work in the Houses of Parliament being rebuilt by Barry. He also carved the lions for the bridge across the Menai Straits. The memorial to Elizabeth Stanhope was produced by Richard Westmacott (1799-1872), who also produced many busts and statues, including one of Archbishop Howley now in Canterbury Cathedral. Jabez Tyley carved the monument to Jane Campbell. His brother Thomas was also a sculptor of both busts and funerary monuments in the early nineteenth century. James Nesfield Forsyth executed the monument to Dean Elliot, who held the appointment from 1850 to 1891. He also produced the monument to Bishop Fraser, the popular Bishop of Manchester, which stands in Manchester Cathedral. J. Paine, who carved the Powell memorial, is also known for his design of the domed chapel on the Gibside Estate in Co Durham. Alfred Drury designed the memorial to Bishop Trelawny.

He was also responsible for the statue of Sir Joshua Reynolds that adorns the entrance to Burlington House. His statuette of Lilith is in the Diploma Gallery of the Royal Academy.

Most of the sculptors in this list are national figures. Along with its architects and glaziers Bristol has used artists of the front rank. Fortunately they sometimes had connections with Bristol as well. They produced a large number of works, but if there was something of a production line the general standard of work is at least as good as anything else to be found in other churches and buildings of the same period.

The monuments to Deans Elliott and Pigou are modelled, clearly, upon those to the abbots located in the Eastern Lady Chapel. These are of the second type of funerary monument to which reference has already been made. The monuments to some of the later bishops are simple slabs, giving the sparse details of their lives. The lettering in all cases is, however, particularly good. Bishop Forrest Browne (1897-1914) is commemorated by an excellent bust executed by Lady Kennet, the widow of the Antarctic explorer Scott. The proportions strike admiration, and the portrayal of character is clearly etched.

The memorials to Catherine Winkworth and Bishop Butler conform to the general style of Victorian presentation. The difference between Southey's effusiveness in the north transept and the more austere earlier commemoration in the Eastern Lady Chapel is particularly noteworthy. The Gothic Revival was also responsible for the reappearance of figured monumental brasses that had been common in the Middle Ages, but which had sometimes used the metal in post-Reformation times. Often they were set in the floor; in Bristol the memorial to Jordan Palmer Palmer is set on a pillar by the south nave aisle pulpit.

These memorials are interesting not only as works of art but as social statements which illuminate the times in which they were set up. They come mostly from the eighteenth and nineteenth centuries. It was during this period that sentiments began to be expressed in word as well as symbol. Though the representations were essentially one-dimensional, with some work in relief, they are accompanied by prose or verse which can often be wordy. Bare factual statements are eschewed. As Dr Johnson said, quite rightly at this time, no man is upon his oath in a lapidary inscription.

There are memorials to those who came to Bristol to take the waters at Hotwells. Spas had become fashionable and Bath was without peer. There was an attempt made to develop Clifton, near the Avon Gorge, along the same lines. It did not succeed, but the memorials remind the viewer of the search for better health and the frequent disappointments that were suffered. With its thriving sugar trade, amongst other commodities, Bristol had close connections with the West Indies and there are reminders of that in the memorials. Edward Colston was one of the great benefactors to the city and also donated to the Cathedral. However, there is no echo anywhere of connections with the infamous slave trade. The houses of the merchants of the time survive. They said nothing of their commercial methods.

To the north were the Thirteen Colonies who sought their independence in the latter part of the century. Not everyone was enthusiastic for the cause. Some had to stay, some emigrated to Canada and some returned to the mother country. There is a memorial to that. Nor was India forgotten, particularly with its army in the nineteenth century. South

Africa appears in an oblique way. The Bishop at the time of the riots was Robert Gray. He was an opponent of reform, though he had a paternal concern for the poor and needy, and sought their welfare when he was the incumbent at Bishop Wearmouth. He had married the daughter of the precentor of Bristol Cathedral and his father-in-law was the mayor. One son was the incumbent at Almondsbury, where he lived after the destruction of the palace. His other son, also called Robert, became Bishop of Cape Town and was responsible for determining the shape and tone of the church of the Province for many years to come.

Theologically, Bishop Joseph Butler is an important figure. He published his *Analogy of Religion* about the time he came to Bristol in 1738. With argument about probability as the basis for evidence and moral obligation, it has continued to be a living influence in English theological thought. Robert Southey, who composed the words for Butler's later memorial, represents the world of literature, as does Catherine Winkworth whose translations of German hymns are still in common use.

Hugh Conway was the pseudonym of Frederick John Fargus; in his day (1847-85) he was one of the country's best-selling novelists. *Called Back* sold 352,000 copies and was translated into most European languages. John Eagles had been curate to Sydney Smith when he held the prebend of Halberton. He resigned his ecclesiastical appointments to give himself over to journalism and literature. He was also an accomplished artist and became known as an art critic, writing for *Blackwood's Magazine*. He also published a more serious work on the Bristol Riots.

J. Havard Thomas produced the lions for the Menai Straits bridge, the entrance piers for Buckingham Palace, and the memorial to Mary Carpenter, a Unitarian. She worshipped at the Lewins Mead chapel where her father was a minister. Her meeting with Ram Mohan Roy widened her horizons and she became interested in India and in the poor, not least in her own country. In 1846 she opened a Ragged School — a place for the non-respectable poor. Other places of education followed and her influence was brought to bear upon the government in Bengal. She was instrumental in setting up colleges for the training of female teachers.

The memorials to these people are perhaps not artistically significant, but they show, along with the others that have also been mentioned, the way in which the life of society flowed through the Cathedral.

Misericords

The furnishings of most interest, however, are the misericords. There are 28, though originally there were 34, which were still in situ in 1788. The movement of the choir stalls during the restoration work, probably about 1860, may well account for their loss. We have no means of knowing what the missing 6 stalls depicted.

The misericords of the abbey have been reset in different woodwork. These tip-up seats date from 1520, within a decade of the commencement of the Henrician Reformation. They are of particular importance for the scenes they portray of the Romance of Reynard the Fox. Like many stories there are variations in the tradition, which inevitably have a bearing on establishing the provenance of any particular expression. This story of the deception of a cock by a fox goes back at least to about 1150 with the publication of the poem *Ysengrimus* by Pierre de Saint Cloud. There is also some connection with the fable Marie de France, with which the poem is contemporaneous. It first appears in English about 1390 in the *Canterbury Tales* of Geoffrey Chaucer, who used it for the *Nun's Priest's Tale*. In between these two dates, two centuries apart, the story may have been dependent upon the oral tradition, which could easily produce variations and sub-themes, not least derived from the life of the farmyard, with which both speakers and hearers would be familiar in a rural society.

When the story came to be told through the medium of the plastic arts other changes took place. The plumage of the cock needs to be conveyed through sharp edging. However, this degree of craftsmanship might not always be available to the workman. The smoother flowing lines of a goose are easier to carve. So, in some cases the goose replaces the cock. Additional sub-themes emerge: the disorganised housewife, marital tensions and animals, somewhat out of control, being driven off by the woman. These touches add a wry humour to the main theme of morality. The preacher in the guise of the fox exhorts his congregation, represented as the cock, to resist temptation, gullibility and vanity. So the clergy perched on their misericords during the time of long services had a constant reminder of both responsibilities and of the constantly available occasions of sin.

The source from which the Bristol carver drew his inspiration is by no means clear. There are various routes and all originate on the mainland of Europe, reaching Bristol in different ways. One suggestion is that it lay through London. However, it is equally plausible to think that the second city of the kingdom, with its extensive trading connections might have had direct access to the source. The evidence for a route through London does not appear very convincing. While it is true that William Caxton had published *The History of Reynard the Fox* in 1481, he did so without printing any illustrations.

Wynkyn de Worde also published something with illustrations that may have been influential. The earliest known version of the romance printed with illustrations was published by Pynson between 1501 and 1505. Unfortunately only part of one woodcut survived so it is difficult to make any assessment of his influence.

Bruin the Bear who features in the portrayals appears as the bear caught in the cleft of a log in *Reynke de Vos*, in an edition of 1498 coming from a Platt Deutsch area, which was also connected with the Netherlands. Bruin also appears in the work of Wynkyn de Worde. Groessinger is led to conclude that the Bristol source comes closest to the Netherlands/Platt Deutsch tradition. Bristol, however, has two presentations of Tibert the Cat attacking the priest and his household. De Worde also has a picture of Reynard going to the gallows. This may be either a German or an English source. There are royal lions and the cat sits atop the gallows. The scenes in which the bear dances with the wolf seem to have no antecedents. Here the carver may have done no more than use prints of animals that were available and could have exercised his imagination upon them. Some creativity on the part of workers is not to be ruled out since the artist is not merely the sum of his sources.

Given, however, that Bristol was a Victorine House which had been founded from

Paris and given, also, the way in which the houses of the order kept in touch with each other regularly through such meetings as General Chapters, some Parisian connection ought to be given serious consideration. About 1500 books of prints were published by Thielmann Kerrer in Paris. Illustrations drawn in the margins of his books seem to inform the designs of the misericords, not only for Reynard but for other themes as well. This French source might be preferred.

Five misericords are important for conveying the story. The crimes of Reynard reached their climax in the rape of the wife of the wolf, Isengrin, and the murder of a number of the cock's relatives. King Noble called Reynard to judgement. Bruin was despatched to bring him to court. However, the bear falls victim to the wiles of the fox, being tempted to search for honey in a half split log which has been wedged open. Bruin looks in, Reynard pulls out the wedge and the bear is trapped. When the villagers hear his calls they come to him, only to beat the bear with rods. A delighted fox looks on, enjoying the scene. Tibert the cat is despatched next. He, too, falls into temptation. He is persuaded to search for mice in the priest's barn, where there is an animal trap; only Reynard knows this. The ensnared cat cries out for help, waking the members of the household who enter the barn to investigate. Tibert in his pain attacks the genitals of the priest. Then the cat is depicted as leaping upon the priest's back. Finally, Grimbert the badger is sent: the friend and cousin of the fox. He is successful. Reynard comes to court, and standing before the King is sentenced to hang. The wolf and the (muzzled) bear dance for joy to the beat of a drum played by an ape. Such rejoicing proves to be premature. Reynard pleads for mercy and, repenting, offers to go on a pilgrimage as an act of penance. The King grants his petition. The fox is spared the gibbet on condition that he goes to the Holy Land and never returns to his native kingdom.

The Bristol misericords vary this tradition by showing Reynard hanged. Geese pull at the ends of the rope and at the fox's tail. The end is foretold in the misericord where the fox is preaching; there is a gallows at the side of the pulpit. Round this basic theme there are the embellishments of comment and humour. The battle of the sexes is prominent. Strife has broken out in the kitchen over the cauldron. The man has been caught in the act of taking food from this cooking pot — he has to learn that the kitchen, in those times, was the domain of the woman, where men enter at their peril. The struggle is likened to a tournament in which the woman is often successful. The female is the eternal temptress personified by Eve, leading her suitors, depicted as apes, to hell. This theme is presented in another Bristol misericord, which draws not only upon Genesis but also on the Wisdom books, where both foolishness and temptation are seductresses. The ape is emblematic of all who fall into these evils, pride and vanity being the supposed characteristics of apes in the mythology of the Middle Ages. Their acts of grooming both themselves and others were taken as signs of the sin of self-adoration. For the baubles of vanity, apes would rob, even violently, as depicted in another misericord. By such actions damnation comes to people. It is the crafty fox who extricates himself.

If the misericords of the Cathedral are important for their presentation of the Romance of Reynard the Fox, they are also noteworthy for their sexual connotations and emphasis upon nudity. There is the temptation in the garden and the consequent expulsion from it; the woman is naked; the man sports prominent genitals. She commands his private parts and thereby controls his virility, which she can now destroy at will. Celibate canons whose sexuality is uncontrolled can fall into sin, transgress and receive punishment. A horse is ridden backwards, showing that sinners suffer by being made ridiculous. The symbolism of the male sinner grasping the horse's tail directs attention to the anus of the stallion, itself a symbol of excessive passion. Sexual activity, in general, was regarded as base in medieval times, but amongst the celibate it was gross sinfulness. It is in this attention to nudity that the influence of the Renaissance can be perceived, since it emphasised once again the human form that the ancients had handled with such perspicacity and grace. For example, in the misericords, nakedness might be required for the portrayal of the scenes in the Garden of Eden. It is hardly necessary for scenes depicting the transport of bears, wrestling and the story of Reynard in general.

At this point one observes the traditional medieval allegorical themes being presented in a different cultural context. Thielmann Kerrer seems to have been the source of this Renaissance influence — another argument for connecting him with the Bristol designs. However, the carver of 1520 had not mastered the new style completely. He was unable to deal accurately and precisely with human anatomy. The mermaid with two devilish monsters, two men running to attack each other and an ape riding upon a mule all seem to come from the same source. The similarity between the carvings and the woodcuts seems clear. The survival of prickmarks is unusual but they do indicate that copying has been done from models.

The Bristol misericords are the product of a lively imagination and constitute a display of artistic competence. While the Renaissance elements may not possess the accuracy of pure classicism, they are vigorously executed and convey their message with panache. In some ways they are rather like the cartoons which appear in newspapers. They convey a truth in an amusing and distorted manner. While it is true that books and prints from a variety of sources may be to hand, a story is told nonetheless. The stories are presented in the context of the lives in which the original viewers lived: like men killing a pig for Christmas, or out hunting, or indulging in wrestling, as the Bristol misericords show.

There is humour, too, of the age in which the scenes were carved. Sometimes it is wry or crude, but the underlying tone is moral rather than pornographic. Our difficulty lies in our attempts to enter into that medieval world with its distinctive symbolism. At first sight the misericords appear as fantastic or grotesque as the gargoyles which are scattered round so many medieval churches. The sceptic might even see some of them as mocking the faith itself. Yet this is not so. Faith and morality are being taught under these forms: the mermaid, the wolf, the bear, the cock, the ape, and, of course, the fox himself are allegorical symbols. Even the emphasis upon nudity and genitalia is a comment, or a reminder, about sexual virtue, not least among celibate canons. The skill lies in finding the key to the symbolism in this foreign world. If this is not done it remains inaccessible at worst; or superficial, crude and naïve at best.

The misericords are not virtuoso art. They are the work of craftsmen, often provincial to the very core, who drew upon what sources they had and fused them with their imagination. The scenes depicted are not obvious when they are not in use, and are equally obscure when they are in use. That is indeed symbolic of their imagery. They have to be sought out. And so they should be, for they are some of the most significant in the country.

North-side misericords, 1-14:

1 Reynard the Fox traps Bruin the bear in the carpenter's yard, looking for honey in the cleft oak.
2 Reynard the Fox watches Tibert the cat caught in a trap whilst looking for mice in the priest's barn.
3 Reynard the Fox goes to the gallows. Tibert the cat ties the rope. Bruin the bear stands behind Reynard as he looks on.
4 Monkeys steal from the pedlar's pack (possibly from the story of Reynard the Fox).
5 Reynard the Fox preaches to the geese, the gallows near.
6 Pig Killing (possibly Guant the pig in the story Reynard the Fox?)
7 Hunting. The hart's horns are caught in a bush.
8 Boy (or Monkey) on camel, with sack as saddle, followed by man holding animal's tail.
9 Reynard the Fox is hanged from the gallows by the geese.
10 Foliage only.
11 Mermaid between two monsters.
12 Adam and Eve.
13 Samson slaying the lion; the jawbone of an ass in his girdle.
14 Two men wrestling using collars: a third man seems to be acting as referee, pointing to a 'foot-fault'.

South-side misericords, 15-28

15 Tilting at the Quintain. A man on a bear thrusting at a full sack held by a large dog (?).
16 An Athletic Contest? Two nudes seated tailor-fashion facing each other on a bench. (Weapons, if any, missing.)
17 Jousting. A man riding a sow versus a woman on a goose (?).
18 A Domestic Quarrel. Woman evidently resenting man's interfering with cooking-pot.
19 Bear and another animal dancing to a drum played by a monkey.
20 Bear muzzled and tethered. Men with wheel-barrow and dogs. Bearbaiting (?) or dancing bear (?).
21 A Devil (?) in the jaws of hell receiving a naked woman who leads on halters four apes.
22 Double-headed Dragon, chasing three naked souls.
23 Fight between man and beast: another beast looks on, holding shield.
24 Slug with Corded Pack on back led on leash by man: another man follows with whip - possibly symbolic of slow transport by pack-horse ("slugs").
25 Nun seated at Lectern, outside building.
26 Man and Woman with Tame Squirrel (possibly from Reynard the Fox; see similar clothes in No.2.)
27 Man (in disgrace) rides face to tail driven on by another on foot.
28 Woman carrying Sack of Corn to Windmill, mounted on a horse.

Roof bosses

If gargoyles demonstrate something of the medieval sense of humour, then roof bosses show the human love of artistry. Ribbed vaults are an important feature of Gothic architecture, and the bosses placed at the crossover point of the ribs are both utilitarian and aesthetic. There are a number of Romanesque bosses to be considered. Stylistic developments suggest that there were at least two teams working on them at different times. The first, with a fondness for beak heads and grotesque masks, laboured in the church. Then a second took over to deal with the chapter house and the gateway. The latter team worked in a non-figurative style and were prone to use repetitive motifs. This second development appears to herald the introduction of the rib vault. By this time architectural development was taking place, with increasing use being made of the pointed arch. The vault in the Elder Lady Chapel is dated to about 1275 where the awkward joints between the walls and the vault are both hidden and strengthened by the use of a wall rib. The main artistic feature of the vaulting is a series of nine bosses. In the easternmost and second bays the bosses have been pushed upwards a little. This makes clear how far the joint is beyond the foliage between the boss and the rib. The fifth boss from the east and in the centre of the chapel shows two dragons biting each other; a fairly recurrent theme throughout the country. The other eight bosses are of foliage, which often consists of six leaves to a boss. The effect is more naturalistic than the foliage on the capitals and spandrels on the walls.

The roof bosses in the Eastern Lady Chapel are of a somewhat later date, though the technique is the same. However, the boss at the centre of each arch tends to be heavier while the minor bosses of the main vault are more complex. At the peak of the second arch from the crossing on the south side, a bearded face has been carved instead of foliage. Perhaps this was the mason's trademark. There are over a hundred faces altogether in the various parts of this eastern section of the Cathedral, but few appear on the bosses. Beside the face just mentioned there is, in this area, only one other on the wall rib above the door from the vestibule into the Berkeley Chapel.

The later period during which Perpendicular Gothic was coming into its own shows both the ornate quality of the vaulting and the bosses. Here there are foliate bosses together with heraldic and figurative ones, located in the north transept. Here there is a random juxtaposition of religious and secular themes with animals and heraldry prominent, in a way which is characteristic of the art of the period.

Inner bay of north transept:
1   The arms of Berkeley. Gules, a chevron between ten crosses patee argent.
2   The arms of the Virgin: a heart pierced by a sword together with wings. These are symbols of the suffering of the Virgin *(Luke 2.v.35)*.
3   Vine and grapes. The vine is often taken to be a symbol of the Eucharist.
4   An eagle. This is heraldic rather than naturalistic. The eagle is the symbol for St John.
5   Three fishes. The origin of this symbol is unknown. The fish was a symbol of faith for early Christians. The intertwining could be an allusion to the Trinity, since the doctrine was sometimes presented by three interlocking symbols.

6   Two saddle bags. No interpretation is possible. It stands in its own right.
7   Two dragons. A common theme used in many places.
8   A dog-headed man. A mythical figure but common in medieval times.
9   Half man and half horse.
10 Half man and half lion.
11 Heraldic rose.
12 Foliage.

Outer bay of north transept:
1   The arms of the passion: the cross and crown of thorns.
2   The passion continued: the column and the scourging.
3   The passion continued: lantern, spear and reed.
4   The arms of the Virgin as above.
5   Heads of three abbots.
6   Four old men with beasts' bodies.
7   Bearded face with two birds. This could be an allusion to Elijah or St Paul the Hermit, both of whom were fed by birds.
8   Two dragons.
9   Two mermaids with a crown.
10 Three bearded faces.
11 Couple with a scroll.
12 A contorted naked king.
13 A contorted clothed king. Restoration work may have clothed this monarch.

These last two bosses have sometimes been thought to commemorate the humiliation of Edward II who, after his forced abdication, was imprisoned at Berkeley Castle. There would seem to be no particular reason why his fate should be represented in art at Bristol after his death, since he had no particular connection with the abbey. Even the tradition that it refused to accept his body for burial appears only in the fifteenth century. If there were hopes of encouraging his cult, which may have been likely at one time, roof bosses are not the obvious place at which to start a shrine for pilgrimage.

The bosses of the nineteenth century nave were designed by Street, and they are executed entirely in foliage. He turned to the Early English style with a clear system of bays, where each vault was punctuated by a sensible set of bosses. The general level of workmanship is good although originality of design and symbol are not to be expected. The carvers worked from the pattern books, owned by them or the supervising architect. The same designs therefore tend to reappear in the churches of the periods concerned. So, for example, the presentation of two dragons biting each other occurs at places as diverse as Wells Cathedral and Iffley Parish Church in Oxford. A bearded face may be that of the mason himself: his distinctive identifying mark, at least for his generation; St Mary's Beverley has the same sort of face in the same position. The arms of the Virgin appear at St Mary Redcliffe. The vine and grapes are also used at Canterbury Cathedral. The issue is not so much creativity as capacity in execution. The Bristol carvers were, clearly, craftsmen of the highest order; and that applies to the Victorians as well. Though the most

56 Misericords.
   Story of
   Reynard the
   Fox: Reynard
   traps Bruin

57 Reynard
   watches the
   trapped Tibert
   the cat

58 Reynard
   preaches

59 The monkeys steal

60 A pig is killed

61 Reynard goes to the gallows

62 Reynard hanged by the geese

63 Bear-baiting

64 Dragon with two heads chasing three nudes

65 Wrestlers

66 Man riding
a horse face
to tail

67 Adam and
Eve with
human-
headed
serpent

interesting bosses are to be found in the north transept, the rarest are the three situated at the entrance to the chapter house, since they are rarely a feature of Romanesque architecture. The later bosses, particularly in the Decorated style, have exquisitely carved foliage. The intended naturalistic effect was not always achieved, but the carver's intention may have been formalistic. In some cases the necessary skill may not have been available, as an apprentice may have tried his hand. There is a boss in the choir where acorns are represented; though if this guess is right, a great deal of imagination is called for. Those who look at roof bosses must do that very often. By their very nature they are obscure and are not viewed easily by the naked eye. Their features are highlighted by colour, but while each individual boss has some individual significance, as in so many cases throughout the churches of the country, there seems to be no overall scheme which we, in our day, can understand.

Domestic wall paintings

The Cathedral is fortunate to possess 13 wall paintings from the old deanery. They were cut from the walls when it was demolished and are now stored in the dorter passage. Most of the designs are framed by a wreath, with texts written in Roman lettering. There is no obvious common theme, and as wall decoration they were no more than entertaining, but are significant as an example of later sixteenth century domestic art. There are elements of fantasy, moralism, the secular and the sacred. Some are in a poor state: the ten-pointed star has a text that is barely recognisable; it may say *Erbut signa*. Parrot talk is satirised with a picture of the bird plus the words *Quod disco dico*. More seriously are a hand reaching out to another hand over a rainbow and a globe with the words *Serua seruabo*: Serve and I will preserve you. Some depict a single scene: a standing male figure with a fallen ass; Balaam and his beast perhaps.

Two have a continuous narrative. The first is of ten virgins with the words *Ecce sponsus benit*: Behold the bridegroom comes. To the right of the wreath are SS Paul and Peter along with King David. Then comes Christ the Good Shepherd (*Periit et inbenta est*: it was lost and is found). The Magdalen kneels. St John Baptist points to the Good Shepherd. Over him there are clouds and angels. Next comes a kneeling figure — perhaps a cleric at prayer. Behind are female figures portraying *Fides, Spes* and *Poenitentia*: Faith, Hope and Penitence; and another set — *Obduratio, Desperatio* and *Metus*: Obstinancy, Despair and Anxiety. Above there is an angel with a sword within the wreath, a hand reaches from a globe, holding a winged heart which is inscribed IHS — above that a hand descends from heaven and seals the heart.

The second portrays Hagar placing Ishmael under a bush, within a circular label ornamented with four bosses inscribed *Audivit Dominus Vocem Pueri*: the Lord heard the voice of the boy. Next is a falling tower again within a circular label, ornamented again with four bosses and inscribed *An Illi Soli Erant Peccatores*: were they alone sinners? Next is Jairus's daughter again in a circular label with the words *Non Obit Mortem Sed Dormit*: she is not dead but sleeping. Finally there is Saul wearing a crown casting a spear at David, again with a circular label and the words *Servavit Davidem Dominus*: the Lord preserved

David. In addition there are, again in wreaths, a hand descending from the clouds holding an anchor on which a crucifix rests upon an open bible. In a mixture of old English and Roman lettering is written *Spe Prece Patientia*: by hope, by prayer and by patience. There are then four females with an anvil and a flaming heart. On the anvil are the words *Non despici cor*. A ship in a storm is guided by a heavenly hand: on the sail there is the inscription *Timebo*; the word 'not' has to be supplied: I shall not be afraid. Then there are two harts, one running and the other lying in a thicket. Here the words are *Secreta mea mihi*. Next, a man holding a pair of scales, together with a medallion showing the head and bust of a female. From a cloud a hand holds a label: *Sufficit tibi gratia mea*: my grace is sufficient for you. Finally, again within a wreath, is an eclipse of the moon showing the sun, the moon and the stars with the inscription *Ascende nitebis*: mount higher and you will shine. Last of all within a round arch, supported on piers built of human bones and skulls, an angel takes the hand of a kneeling man. The inscription is *Mors vitae ianva*: death the gateway to life.

Clearly the dormitory of the old deanery held much of iconographic interest.

7 Stained glass

On entry to the Cathedral there are three dominant impressions: one of space, one of light, and a third of stained glass which belongs to the period 1930-50. The production of space has been examined in the chapter dealing with the rebuilding of the nave. The first and third impressions are closely related. The artificial lighting, installed only in the 1990s, is indirect and aims to heighten the structural features. The natural light is the result of the careful use of clear glass which serves as a frame for the various figures and themes set in the large late Gothic style windows designed by Street.

There has been a good deal of restoration work done to the glass, but on the whole it has been done effectively and with sensitivity. This work was carried out during the nineteenth century and after the 1939-45 war, during which the Cathedral was damaged. A good deal of the damage resulted from bomb blasts, which harmed the windows in particular. However, there is a good deal of medieval stained glass in the building, and it is with this that we begin.

The most important and most dramatic of the medieval stained glass is to be found in the large window at the east end, which it dominates. It dates from the mid-fourteenth century but has been restored during the nineteenth century and post-1945 period. The window has a clear theme: the Tree of Jesse. It aims to convey the descent of Jesus from Jesse, the father of David, who established the monarchy of his house. After the fall of Jerusalem the house fell from view but later, after the return from Babylon and over a period of time, the idea of a Davidic Messiah came to the fore. Christians saw that fulfilled in the ministry of Jesus of Nazareth. The theme of the window, therefore, conveys the 'theological credentials' of Jesus validating the Christian claim. *(Isaiah ch.11 v.1; Acts ch.13 vv.22-23)*.

The theme is set out in 21 sections. In the bottom half there are nine main lights. To north and south there are six lights, three on either side, in which are placed 12 prophets. They are placed in two rows and while they adopt various poses, all of them incline to the centre. In those central three windows are two pairs of kings on either side of Jesse, who occupies the central lower space. Above him stands the Madonna and Child. In the centre of the entire window is the portrayal of the Crucifixion based upon the Johannine account. *(John ch.19 vv.25-27)*. The scene is presented in the form of a triptych: The Blessed Virgin in the north light, Jesus in the centre and St John to the south.

The tracery openings above the nine prophetic-regal lights and to north and south of the triptych contain a variety of heads, kings and prophets together with a number of hooded men. Finally at the top, towards the apex, are heraldic signs which are significant in their own right but are also important as evidence for dating the window. The evidence for the dating does not rest, however, merely upon the heraldry; style is also significant.

The Bristol window should be placed alongside the French windows to be found in the Abbey of St Denis near Paris and datable to *c*1144, as well as with those of Chartres, which are of the same period (*c*1115-55). The Tree of Jesse is presented in them through three lancet windows:

       1 Prophets   2 Kings   3 Prophets.

York Minster and Canterbury Cathedral have this same conventional arrangement, indicating an earlier date from the window design. Bristol with its late Decorated/Early Perpendicular window is later. The greater single space permitted elaboration and a greater coherence of theme.

Later developments seem to be apparent at Carlisle and Selby. The Augustinian cathedral at Carlisle suffered great damage to its Jesse window. Enough fragments survive, in Smith's judgement, to show that the same glazier did not execute the window for both Bristol and Carlisle. However, each house may have been aware of what the other was doing. That of course is not surprising, since they both belonged to different parts of the same religious order.

The Tree window at Selby Abbey has been restored more than once, but the features appear to have remained the same. There are seven lights:

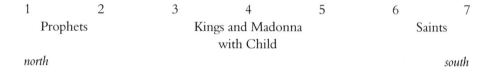

1	2	3	4	5	6	7
Prophets			Kings and Madonna		Saints	
			with Child			
north						*south*

The general arrangement is not dissimilar from Bristol, and both point to a somewhat later date.

There are three windows produced by Thomas of Oxford about 1380. The window at Gloucester Cathedral has been scattered. Fragments are to be found in the east window of the Lady Chapel. There are other remains in the first window of the southern choir at York Minister, and the third in a much restored and rearranged form is to be found at Winchester College. What remains seems to confirm that date for the Bristol window.

Perhaps the most compelling evidence is to be found in a group of eight windows that appear to have been produced by a single glazier, whose name is unknown. All are Tree of Jesse and the locations are Lowick, Ludlow, Madley, Mancetter, Merevale, Shrewsbury, and Tewkesbury, with Bristol as the eighth. They have common features of design: vines with trefoil leaves, vines that curl round the figures. Some have birds in the foliage, but this is not the case with Bristol, which has a monkey-like animal. (Now relocated in the cloisters). All use deeply coloured glass with a diaper of quatrefoils (again to be found in the cloisters). The arrangements at Bristol, Ludlow and Shrewsbury are much the same, with prophets on the outer areas and kings in the inner. Both Bristol and Ludlow make use of hooded men, bearded and sometimes crowned. Particular use is made of them in the rather awkward openings in the tracery. This group of eight seems to be related and also appears to be somewhat later than the York window, which means a date after *c*1310.

If the heraldry is then taken into account Sabin's argument for a date mid-century seems sustainable. Further, as this heraldic glass at the top of the window does not seem ever to have been disturbed, it may be taken as decisive for the dating of the window as a whole.

However, the style of the royal arms in the window may enable us to be a little more precise. The arms displayed are those in use from about 1195 until 1340. They were then quartered with the *fleur de lys* of France and used on the Great Seal. Thus heraldry was used to assert the claim of Edward III to the throne of France. Assuming that the canons and the workmen knew of this change, then the glass should have been made by 1340, which would bring the date forward by a few years.

The restoration work falls into two sections: nineteenth century and post-1945. The extent of the restoration for the nineteenth century is aided by the water colours painted by Winston before the work was carried out. Records show the twentieth-century work. Broadly speaking the figures in the lower half of the window have been restored whilst the upper half has remained largely untouched. The pattern appears in **28**.

Some fragments of the original glass which could not be used in the restoration work may well lie as individual pieces in the cloister windows. Overall there is a clear impression of a fourteenth-century window design. Further, it seems as though the various restorations have been done faithfully and sensitively. There was no choice but to restore if the window was to remain *in situ*. The only other course was to remove it either wholly or partially. The result of the restoration work justifies the course that was taken.

The popularity of the theme is displayed not only in the use made of it by sculptors in places like Lichfield, Hereford and Westminster; it is also used by painters and the makers of vestments, like copes, at Exeter, Canterbury and St Paul's, London. It also features on monumental reredoses in such places as St Cuthbert's, Wells. More significantly, for Bristol, is its use in manuscripts. The Augustinian abbey had a psalter datable *c*1270 in which the Tree of Jesse appears though the presentation is different from the window. The psalter only reappeared relatively recently, and is now in the Library of Krivoklat Castle, Prague, in the Czech Republic.

The window high above the entry to the Elder Lady Chapel contains late medieval glass, placed there on the eve of the Reformation during the time of Abbot Elyot (1515-26). This still has the original glass, in good condition, in the tracery. This window may be thought to hold a sparkling, yet typical, medieval set, with backgrounds of red and blue. The four main lights there are a rich miscellany of fragments. These include canopy work, faces, broken inscriptions and quarries of patterns the same as those in the cloister, where they can be studied more conveniently. Basically there is a programme suitable for the entrance to a Lady Chapel, dedicated as it is to the Blessed Virgin Mary. The Annunciation and the Coronation are portrayed. Orthodoxy is protected by the Father holding the Crucifix of his Son. The Trinity and the Virgin are related to the witness borne to them by the Evangelists, while SS Peter and Paul make oblique reference to the Holy See, founded by them according to tradition. There was an allegiance here to more than the Tudor monarchy.

Henry VIII, Edward VI and Elizabeth I presided over a period of religious change in which iconoclasm was a major feature. This destructiveness came to its climax during the Republic and Protectorate. One is surprised that so much survived troubled times. The

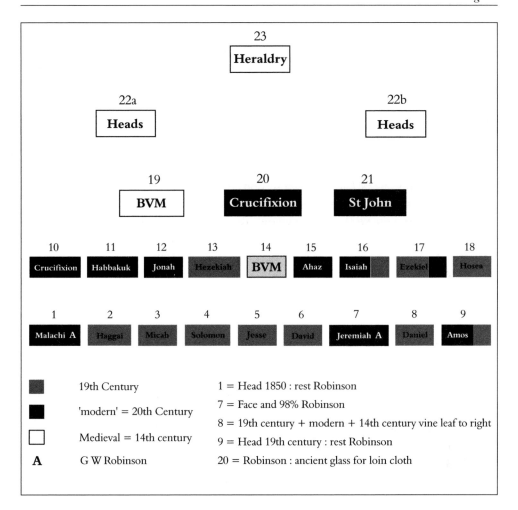

68 Plan of Jesse window

Restoration of the Monarchy in 1660 started to reverse these devastations. Two windows were placed at the east end of both the north and south choir aisles. The heraldry suggests that they were installed by Dean Henry Glemham who was in Bristol between 1660 and 1667. There was a tradition that the windows were actually donated by Nell Gwynne, one of Charles II's mistresses. However, Samuel Pepys declared that he was a relative of Barbara Castlemaine, the dominant mistress in the immediate period after the Restoration. Despite the fact that there was a notice in the Cathedral during the eighteenth century (now lost) to say that the windows had been donated by Mistress Gwynne, it is probably safer to ascribe this to local tradition rather than to established fact. Glemham's heraldry seems to support a straightforward and less sexual interpretation.

Much of the interest in the windows is technical. It was during the seventeenth century that enamelling was used to create windows. The technique had been known for some time and was used when complicated details had to be executed; for example with heraldic symbols. Traditionally windows had been made up of small pieces of coloured glass; with this process larger pieces of glass could be used and required colour could be added. However, when Louis XIV invaded Lorraine, the main source of supply, the glass furnaces, were destroyed and no more glass could be obtained from that source. However, the technique was known elsewhere and if the windows were in place before 1668, then it would seem that the technique had been handled in Bristol, (or at least in England), in which case we have here an example of pioneering work. The destruction of the Lorraine furnaces was after 1667, when Glemham moved to St Asaph as bishop.

The window in the south choir aisle was destroyed by bomb blast on November 24 1940. Fortunately both windows had been painted by J. Manning in 1826. From his picture we can describe the lost window. It consisted of three panels:

The Annunciation	Expulsion of the money changers	Peter and the fish holding the tribute
Gideon's Fleece	Jacob's dream	Abraham and Melchizedek.

The fragments that survived the blast were assembled in a band across the four lights of the easternmost side windows in the south choir aisle.

The portrayals in the surviving window are:

The agony in the garden	The Resurrection	Ascension of Jesus
The sacrifice of Isaac	Jonah and the great fish	Ascension of Elijah.

The six panels constitute a display of typology; a significant event in the life of Jesus finds its type in an Old Testament event. In some cases the comparison is easy: Ascension and burial —resurrection; tribute — giving of gifts, the sacrifice of the son; the action of the spirit. In other cases it is less so. Those with sensitive political antennae may see something of Anglican Royalist triumphalism here. Salvation is portrayed as being wrought by the faithful few (Gideon); the Lord brings judgement (money changers). Payment is to be made to rulers (Peter). This must be conjecture. There seems to be nothing to hint at a contribution by Nell Gwynne (or Barbara Castlemaine). The typology seems biblical and the heraldry Glemham's.

The seventeenth century also saw a large window inserted into the West wall of the truncated Cathedral. This was the gift of Bishop Robert Wright (1623-32). It appears to have five lights with tracery above. Prints also show windows north and south of this with two ranks of four lights, plus quatrefoil tracery in each window. Whether these two windows ante-dated the Wright window or were contemporary with it is unclear. There is no mention of further windows being introduced into the west wall after the episcopate of Bishop Wright. They must be before Wright, in the which case the centre of the wall was windowless; or they are contemporary with the centre window, in the which case the report of Wright's contribution understates the size of his munificence. All disappeared when the nave was rebuilt. There is no knowledge of the nature of the glazing.

The Romantic Movement discovered what we now call Medieval times: the term is one invented in the nineteenth century. It may also be described as the Gothic Revival. Many aspects of life were affected: architecture, with bold designs like Manchester Town Hall, or suburban villas in North Oxford; there were pointed arches everywhere. Novels were described as 'Gothic', and medieval churches were restored by those who thought that, at last, the Middle Ages could be understood. Stained glass could not escape and it did not. In order to understand the movement as a whole and in particular, we must be clear about what was being attempted. From one point of view it could not be considered creative at all; rather it was imitative. The artists rejoiced in their capability to execute what they thought their medieval forebears accomplished. No doubt some of it was pastiche but other work had the spark of a new creation, even if the 'vocabulary' seemed antiquarian.

The nineteenth-century stained glass in Bristol Cathedral is remarkable for that freshness. Where medieval glass has been restored, the work has been done with sensitivity and apparent regard for the original. The glass, which is wholly nineteenth century, has the same quality about it. We shall need, therefore, to distinguish between the nineteenth-century work of restoration and the original glass of the same period found in the Cathedral choir (east of the present nave pulpit), and the glass in the present nave which, of course, post-dated its building in the last third of the nineteenth century. The spirit of the Gothic revival lived on well beyond the death of Victoria in 1901. In many ways it continued through the first third of the twentieth century, and it will be useful to take this entire period as a whole.

The north-east and the north-west windows of the Eastern Lady Chapel contain significant work by Bell, *c*1850, even though there is a little fourteenth-century work in the transom and parts of the three shields. The four Evangelists are portrayed. SS Luke and John were damaged during the 1939-45 war and were restored by Woore. The south-east window is also mainly nineteenth-century, but based on fourteenth-century originals. It too was damaged severely by bomb blast. The south-west window is of the same kind: nineteenth-century based on fourteenth-century originals.

The Newton Chapel's east window has glass executed by W.E. Tower and the south window is by Bell. On the north side of the Cathedral in the Elder Lady Chapel all the glass is Victorian. The glass in the nave and west towers is all nineteenth-century or later. The first window in the aisle, at the easternmost end, was designed by Street, the nave architect, and the work was carried out by Hardman. The next two windows were executed by G.J. Hunt and the last one, again, was designed by Street and made by Hardman. The windows of the towers together with the great rose window make up a good sequence of late-Victorian glazing. On the whole the coloration is richer — stronger, perhaps — on the south than on the north.

We may note some change of emphasis in the themes portrayed in this nineteenth-century glass. The Reformation has taken its toll. The Blessed Virgin still appears, but with perhaps less prominence than in the fourteenth century. The four Evangelists find a place in the schema and so does biblical typology. This is evident in Street's work; for example Melchizedek brings forth bread and wine *(Genesis ch.14 v.18)* paralleled by Jesus' action at Cana *(John ch.2 vv.1-11)*; Rebecca comes to Isaac *(Genesis ch.24 v.63)* paralleled with the arrival of the bridegroom in the Parable of the Wise and Foolish Bridesmaids *(Matthew ch.25)*. In some cases the comparisons may be thought somewhat far-fetched, but the designer has sought clearly to locate presentations of the Christian Faith in a precise biblical context.

There is also a greater sense of church history in the subjects chosen for the windows, as well as characters in the history of the Abbey, Cathedral and city. This is particularly evident in the east window of the Newton Chapel where eight abbots appear, plus St Augustine of the Gregorian Mission preaching on College Green. This appears to be an echo of the meeting that he had with St David on an unknown site in the district. Present devotions locate it at Aust; College Green is just as plausible. The south window of the south transept depicts Robert Fitzharding, the founder of the Abbey, his wife Eva, and his great benefactor King Henry II. The window in the south-west tower portrays the Fathers of the Church: SS Ambrose, Athanasius, John Chrysostom and Jerome. If Bristol public opinion would not allow them to be shown as statues in the porch they could be shown, perhaps more reticently, in the stained glass. The balancing north-west window contains the major prophets. The rose window shows Christ in majesty, together with the musicians of the heavenly host and personifications of the fine arts: painting, navigation, justice and welfare.

In 1910 it was believed there were 14 Victorian windows in the Cathedral. Others were added in the same style, but much was lost in the 1939-45 war. Only eight survived. We shall examine restoration presently. First we would do well to recognise the artistry and craftsmanship of these nineteenth-century workmen. Bristol was one of the major glass-making centres in the country and had the expertise to match. Joseph Bell (1810-95) had his workshop on College Green, which must have been most convenient, since he is a major contributor of nineteenth-century glass.

Bell began work at the Cathedral in 1840, the year he founded his business, and had a further spell there between 1852 and 1853. At this stage the rediscovery of the art of making stained glass was relatively unsophisticated. There is some roughness initially, but by the time that the later nineteenth century is reached the production methods and artistic styles had come to fruition.

The north-east window of the Eastern Lady Chapel is a case in point. The glass in the lower part appears harsh. Smith thought that the purple was 'abrasive' and that the bearded faces appeared very Victorian. There is, perhaps, a certain fullness of face that is rarely observed in medieval glass. Smith also considered that the drapery, which seemed to be imitating a fourteenth-century style, also lacked conviction. The same might be said of some of the figures in the lower part of the Tree of Jesse window. However, Smith does point out that when the Victorians had something definite to work on, like medieval fragments, they were more confident and therefore often more successful.

What is somewhat more mystifying is the decision of the craftsmen to relocate windows. Sometimes it was probably in order to make the best of a bad job, where the glass had deteriorated. In other circumstances it was clearly designed to show the old glass to advantage. Thus it appears as though it was decided to locate the best of the figurative glass on the south side of the Eastern Lady Chapel because the light was better there, as indeed it is. For example, the Martyrdom of St Edmund was placed there. While it is true that much is of the nineteenth century, the lower part of the body is, in all probability, fourteenth-century. The rest appears to be nineteenth-century, but again, based upon fourteenth-century designs. With the Berkeleys, knights and ecclesiastics this triptych is one of the most interesting and successful pieces of stained glass in the Cathedral.

The work of Hardman working to the designs of Street is of particular significance. Street devised carefully thought out schemes; one on biblical typology and the other on the efficacy of prayer. Hardman intended to convey them symbolically by the use of dense coloration, and blue in particular. The impact of this coloration has now been lost to a certain extent, because one window was moved and there was also the removal of some glass. The glass of the Elder Lady Chapel conveys something of the quality of his work. The east window conveys the theme of the Magnificat in five panels: Annunciation, Presentation, Nativity, and then, on a lower level, the Fall of the Rebel Angels and God dealing with Abraham. The original decor of the Chapel was blue, the traditional colour for Our Lady. It has now been replaced by the more celebratory colours of gold and red to give warmth on the north side.

For his work Street preferred to keep to a group of craftsmen in whom he had confidence. As far as stained glass was concerned, he often used Bell and fairly frequently Hardman. This is evident from the glass in Bristol Cathedral. Joseph Bell had undertaken work there before Street was commissioned. Alfred Bell was more his contemporary. He also worked for G.G. Scott and J.L. Pearson. Kempe was also one of his pupils and also worked on the stained glass in Bristol Cathedral.

Of the other major makers of stained glass for the Cathedral, Charles Eames Kempe carried on the tradition of his master, Alfred Bell. In time he founded his own company. His earlier work suffered in reputation since he did not sign it. His later work with its characteristic cartouche is better known and secures his reputation. He was a Tractarian, and worked with William Morris in the Arts and Craft Movement. He was drawn towards fifteenth-century English and Flemish design and coloration: subdued, with intricate detail and the use of silver stain. Like Street and many other artists of the time he thought that the highest art had its spring in religion. Street took much the same view, but thought, nonetheless, that medieval workmen were craftsmen who did their work and ate their food at the breaks, without flying into spiritual realms of mystical vocation. The religion lay in doing the job well.

Walter Ernest Tower makes a modest contribution to the glass of the Cathedral. In a sense he finished off Kempe's work, for he was his nephew. Having been made a partner he took over his uncle's company on his death in 1907.

Though a number of windows were not installed in the nineteenth century, they were executed in the same idiom. The designs are by G.J. Hunt and the work was carried out by A. Saulsby. The portrayals are obvious and relate to the war service given between 1914 and 1918 by the RNVR Bristol Division. Use is made of famous Bristolians in the windows, like Edward Colston, or 'honorary' Bristolians like John Cabot, together with famous national sailors like Francis Drake, Robert Blake, Horatio Nelson and Walter Raleigh. The first and last echo the writings of Richard Hakluyt who was a Residentiary Canon in the seventeenth century. These windows were installed in the inter-war period.

There were further windows on the same theme of commemorating war service after the 1939-1945 war. These portray the Home Guard, the Air Raid Warden Service, the Police, the Red Cross, the Fire Service, St John's Ambulance, and the Nursing Service. In the transom are the dates of the major air raids over Bristol. Faith, hope and love crown the whole. This work was executed by Arnold Wathen Robinson who played a major rôle in the installation of the twentieth-century stained glass. They are in the same idiom as those of the earlier period; indeed so exact are the faces, in some cases, that after they were installed viewers were able to recognise by name some of the faces that were portrayed. Hence there is more than an element of realism in the lights, which reflect the service given to Bristol by the Voluntary Services during severe bombing. However, though art has been used to commemorate, sentimentality has been avoided.

Robinson was also responsible for other windows, like those in the Berkeley Chapel. They are in the same style. Robinson was a Bristol craftsman born of a well-established family in the city in 1888. After attending Clifton College he went to London where he was the pupil of Christopher Whall, who espoused the artistic styles of William Morris and Sir Edward Burne-Jones. In 1913 he set up his own business and built up his reputation by designing and making the stained glass windows in the chapel of the Bristol Royal Infirmary and the Baptist Theological College (now the Department of Archaeology in the University of Bristol), together with windows in Henbury and Westbury Park parish churches. In 1923 he bought out the old-established firm of Joseph Bell and Son which had received commissions from the Cathedral in the past. This business was situated conveniently near to the Cathedral at 12 College Green. Later he became a partner in the Bristol Guild of Applied Arts and, later still, the sole controller. The business and the Guild were then relocated at 68-70 Park Street. During the 1939-45 war Robinson served as an Air Raid Warden, so that in many ways he was qualified, in every respect, to make the Civil Defence windows in the Cathedral, which are executed in his mature sparse style: a far cry from the luscious idiom of thirty years before. These later windows may be considered as his finest work.

Historic cathedrals rarely have the opportunity to incorporate modern art into their total schema. Bristol is no exception. There is but one window of a contemporary design, made in 1965. If critics have often been dismissive of Gothic fantasy and imitativeness they are sometimes bewildered by the abstract symbolism of modern art. Keith New's window at the east end of the south choir aisle has no inscription, but he did supply explanatory notes to the chapter. He drew attention to the long vista enjoyed by the location of the window, even though the window space itself is not large. That, however, is compensated for in that the window stands in relative isolation from other windows. New saw this as a challenge to produce something that would read coherently from a distance, but with sufficient detail to hold interest when studied close-up. At the same time the twin window in the north choir aisle was sufficiently powerful in its colours to require them also to be taken into account: blue, green, red, yellow and white.

New chose the theme of the Holy Spirit and then presented the third person of the Trinity across the whole range of creation, rather than choosing to concentrate merely upon aspects of the Persona. Thus the lower part of the window presents the Spirit as Creator, as described in Genesis chapters 1 and 2. The main image that dominates the centre of the window seeks to convey the power of the Spirit, through fire and holiness. The brilliant red square aims, therefore, to convey the dramatic events of Pentecost *(Acts ch.2 vv.1-4)*. Finally the tracery presents the sevenfold gifts of the Spirit: Wisdom, Understanding, Counsel, Strength, Knowledge and Piety together with the Fear of the Lord. The representation is through seven lamps, each a burst of jewelled light. The total conception was one of simplicity, which appealed through colour, and the spatial relationships between the parts to appeal to the emotions and to intuition, rather than to an intellectual analysis of the symbolism conducted consciously.

The artist came to this task a decade after he produced some of the windows in the nave of the new Coventry Cathedral, which is the modern Anglican cathedral *par excellence.* Here at Bristol he was most constrained: not only was the building old, but he was required to fit his design into the shape of a fourteenth-century window. This is an unusual framework for a modern artist since devising a presentation in the form of a triptych is not simple. The range of colour, the varying texture of the glass and the sheer dynamism of the design carry off the symbolism of the Holy Spirit very well. Smith points out that the effect is heightened by the natural light in the morning when the sun shines directly through the window. Whether New had this in mind when he designed the window is unlikely, perhaps, but it adds much to both the vitality and symbolism of the Creator Spirit, with the Sun of Righteousness and the echo of the Resurrection.

Like most historic churches there has been a good deal of restoration work, but on the whole this has been well done with sensitive attention to the originals. The conventional memorials in glass from both the nineteenth and twentieth centuries aim more at verisimilitude than at symbolism. They are statements of appreciation. The most modern piece of glass is convincing, and throughout its history the Abbey and Cathedral have used local craftsmen of competence and vision, who remembered, too, that modesty was a mark of the Augustinian Order.

Window references and dates

I	fourteenth *c.* R. AWR.
N2	nineteenth & twentieth *c.* B. W.
N3	
S2	nineteenth *c.*
S3	nineteenth *c.* fourteenth Or.
N4	seventeenth *c.* R. nineteenth & twentieth *c.*
S4	twentieth c. K New.
S5	seventeenth c. R.
S9	nineteenth / 20th c. WET.
S10	nineteenth c.
S11	nineteenth c. ?
S12	nineteenth c. CEK.
N10	sixteenth c. Or.
N11	seventeenth c. R.
N12	nineteenth c.
S13,	14, 15, 16, 17, 18
N13,	14, 15, 16, 17
W1, 2, 3	

All nineteenth century ★

Berkeley Chapel:
twentieth c. AWR.
S1, 2, 3, 4.
S5, 6, 7 : some ancient glass.
Elder Lady Chapel
N1, 2, 3, 4, 5 H

★In detail:

S13	SH
S14	GJH & AS
S15	also
S17	S & H
S18	H
W3	H
N13–16	AWR
N17	H.

Key:

AWR:	A.W. Robinson
AS:	A. Saulsby
B:	J. Bell
WET:	W.E. Tower
CEK:	C.E. Kempe
H:	Hardman
S:	Street
W:	Woore
c:	century
R:	Restored
O:	Original.

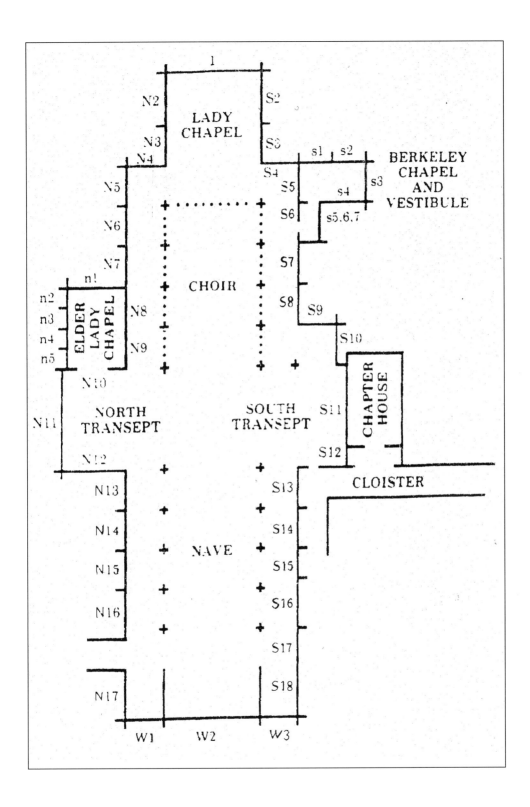

Glossary

Abbey	The buildings and lands of a monastic and Augustinian community.
Abbot	The head and leader of a monastery.
Aisle	A side area of a church, running parallel to the nave *(qv)* and sometimes of the choir *(qv)*, being separated from them by arcading *(qv)*.
Altar	A table-like object on which the sacred vessels, bread and wine are placed during a service of Holy Communion.
Apse	A semi-circular or oval protrusion from the wall of a church, usually at the East end.
Arcade	A series of arches supported on columns.
Augustinians	A religious order made of canons *(qv)* known as Canons Regular; that is clergy observing a common rule. They were not monks in the strict sense of the word, but are treated generally as such. The order developed during the tenth and eleventh centuries as priests started to live in community and take their inspiration from the communities which St Augustine of Hippo organised. *See also Victorines and Bonhommes.*
Austin	A common contraction of the word Augustinian.
Baroque	A style of architecture mainly seventeenth century and of Italian origin; used in England in the later seventeenth and early eighteenth century. The style is dramatic, handling a mass of material whilst at the same time seeking to 'involve' their viewer.
Benedictines	A monastic order following the Rule of St Benedict of Monte Cassino.
Bishop	An old English word for the Greek episkopos = Superintendent; the first order of clergy, usually in charge of a diocese = the area of responsibility.
Bonhommes	A small religious community associated with the Augustinians.

	Bishop Paul Bush, first Bishop of Bristol, belonged to this order.
Boss	An ornamental projection at the intersection of the ribs of a vault.
Buttress	A mass of material placed against the outer wall of a building to counteract the outward thrust.
Byzantine	Relating to the life, worship, art and architecture of the Eastern Roman Empire based on Constantinople built on the site of Byzantium, now Istanbul.
Capital	The upper part of a column.
Canon	**(a)** Canon Regular: a priest in a community who observed the rule of the order. **(b)** Canon Residentiary: a member of a cathedral chapter *(qv)* who is required to keep certain periods of residence. **(c)** Minor Canon: a clerical member of a cathedral who is not a member of chapter.
Cassock	A full-length garment worn underneath liturgical garments and/or ordinary working dress for the clergy.
Cathedral	A church where the Bishop *(qv)* has his teaching chair or throne.
Chancel	The area of a church located eastwards from a screen or step, including the choir stalls and altar.
Chapter	The managing group of clergy in a cathedral or monastery.
Chapter house	The place where the chapter meets.
Charnel house	The place where the bones of deceased members of the community were kept.
Chevron	A zig-zag or continuously repeated V-shaped moulding. In heraldry an inverted V motif.
Choir	The area of a church east of the nave containing choir stalls and extending to the sanctuary where the altar is placed.
Classical architecture	A style derived from those of ancient Greece and Rome.
Clerestory	The uppermost storeys of a church lit by windows; so called because the storey is clear of the roofs of the aisle *(qv)*.
Clerk	Short for Clerk in Holy Orders, the legal definition of an Anglican clergyman and used generally in medieval times.

145

Cloister	The walkway and working area of a monastery/abbey, usually in the form of a square or rectangle at the centre of the buildings complex.
Corbel	A projection from a wall, often carved.
Cosmati	A type of ornamental work, usually on the ground, practised by the Italian family of the same name; imitated later by others like Pearson.
Cruciform	In the shape of a cross; a common plan for a church.
Cusp	The point made by the intersection of the curves of tracery; often moulded, sometimes decorated by a flower design.
Deacon	The third of the major orders of the church (bishop, priest, deacon); the assistant to the celebrant at a Holy Communion service/Mass *(qv)*. Sub-deacon: fourth order; the second assistant at Mass.
Dean	The leader and chairman of a cathedral chapter *(qv)*.
Decorated	A later form of Gothic *(qv)* architecture characterised by considerable elaboration.
Diaper	An overall pattern of carved or painted motifs; generally in small squares or diamonds = lozenges.
Dissolution	The abolition of the monastic houses and abbeys of England by Henry VIII during the later 1530s.
Dorter	A dormitory.
Early English	An early form of Gothic *(qv)* architecture of simplicity, with pointed arches and lancet windows, sometimes grouped in three.
Episcopal	See bishop.
Eucharist	The anglicisation of the Greek word for *Thanksgiving* which is the central prayer of the Holy Communion service; used of the service as a whole.
Evensong	The Anglican service of evening prayer, composed from the monastic offices of Vespers and Compline.
Finial	An ornament which tops another ornament, e.g. at the top of a pinnacle.
Foil	Small arc openings in the tracery of a window. Trefoil=three; Quatrefoil=four.

Gargoyle	A spout whose end has often been carved in a grotesque manner, often a human face.
Gothic	A form of architecture common in Europe during medieval times and the later nineteenth century; particularly dominant between the thirteenth and sixteenth centuries. Divided, usually, into Early English, Decorated and Perpendicular *(qv)*.
Haketon	A garment made of cloth for use under chain mail.
Harrowing of Hell	A description of the descent into hell, according to the Christian creed, by Christ, to save the souls languishing there.
Hauberk	A long coat of chain mail.
Iconography	The study of artistic symbols, especially of human forms as statues.
Lady Chapel	A side chapel of a church, dedicated to the Blessed Virgin Mary.
Liturgy	An anglicisation of the Greek word for service; now meaning the order of a church service.
Mass	An anglicisation of the Latin word *missa,* used to dismiss the congregation at the end of a Communion service.
Matins	The Anglican form of morning prayer, adapted from the monastic office.
Mitre	The pointed headgear of a bishop and some abbots when acting liturgically or ceremonially.
Misericord	A tip-up seat, generally carved, against which a monk or canon could rest during the recitation of an office.
Monastery	The buildings and land of a religious community of monks. See also abbey.
Nave	The main part of a church where the congregation sits.
Palladian	A type of architecture used by A Palladio, an Italian, whose style was introduced into England by Inigo Jones in the early seventeenth century.
Passion	From the Latin *passio* meaning suffering; applied to the sufferings of Christ.
Perpendicular	The last stage of Gothic *(qv)* architecture, marked by elaborate decoration, fan vaulting, slim columns and use of much glass.

Pier	Material massed together to withstand the downward pressure of a building; usually massive in scale.
Pilaster	A shallow rectangular part column projecting to a greater or lesser extent from a wall.
Piscina	A basin with a drain, usually near an altar, used for washing vessels and hands.
Poleyn	Armour protecting the knees.
Postern	A back door or gate; a private entrance and exit.
Prebendary	The holder of a prebend, part of the income available to a cathedral.
Precentor	A priest, usually a canon, who has responsibility for music and worship.
Prior	The second leader of a monastery or abbey.
Pulpitum	The screen at the entrance to the choir, often solid, but open sometimes as at Bristol; on it might stand the organ and in medieval times the rood screen *(qv)*.
Reredos	The screen behind the altar.
Rococo	A development of Palladian *(qv)* architecture pre-dating the Neo-Classical period; mainly an interior style.
Romanesque	A style of architecture, sometimes known as Norman; characterised by heavy pillars, round arches and geometric carvings.
Roll	A document rolled: giving details of matters of administration.
Rood	A group of figures: Jesus on the cross, with the Blessed Virgin on one side and St John on the other; often placed on the pulpitum *(qv)*. Removed at the Reformation but restored in some cases during the Catholic Revival.
Rose window	Sometimes known as a wheel window; a large circular window.
Sacrist	A monastic and cathedral official responsible for the care of the sacred vessels and objects, especially in relation to worship.
Sarum	The Latin form of Salisbury. Sarum rite = the order of services used there, and in common use in medieval England.
Sedilia	Seating; from the Latin for seating.

Slype	A passage between walls; commonly used for a walkway from a cloister *(qv)*.
Soffits	The under surface of an architectural feature.
Surcoat	A medieval outer garment, often sleeveless and with heraldic symbols.
Temporale	A book which gives details of the variable parts of religious services, eg. for saints' days.
Tithe	Ten percent of the value of an item, which was to be given to the church for its upkeep.
Tracery	A pattern formed in a window by the intersection of window bars; usually made of stone holding the glass.
Transept	The arm of a church placed at right angles to the nave and choir *(qv)*.
Triforium	A gallery or arcade above the arches of the nave and choir *(qv)*.
Tympanum	The area enclosed by the lintel of a door and the arch.
Vault	An arches roof. Rib vault: the projecting stones of a vault giving, collectively, the impression of a rib cage.
Victorines	A part of the Augustinian Order *(qv)* based on the Abbey of St Victor, named after him, near Paris.
Visitation	A formal examination of the life and work of a church.

Bibliography and notes

St Augustine's Abbey: Note on Sources

Few medieval records relating to St Augustine's Abbey survive. Most notable is the Cartulary or list of properties belonging to the abbey which was compiled in the thirteenth century. This has been edited by Canon David Walker and is listed below. Abbot Newland's Roll also provides much information. There are a few late-medieval accounts and manorial records, while some leases of abbey properties are preserved in the Bristol Record Office. Several of the bishops' registers for the diocese of Worcester have been printed by the Worcestershire Historical Society. Notes on other surviving records were made by F S Hockaday and are among the invaluable collection of his Abstracts in the Gloucester Public Library. The successive Transactions of the Bristol and Gloucestershire Archaeological Society from 1876 also contain many useful articles and references, as do the Annual Reports of the Friends of Bristol Cathedral. The following works also provide major sources of information:

Beachcroft, Gwen & Sabin, Arthur eds. *Two Compotus Rolls of Saint Augustine's Abbey*, Bristol, Bristol Record Society, IX, 1938

Bettey, Joseph *The Suppression of the Religious Houses in Bristol*, Bristol Historical Association, 1990

Bettey, Joseph *St Augustine's Abbey, Bristol*, Bristol Historical Association, 1996

Britton, J. *The History and Antiquities of Bristol Cathedral*, 1836

Dickinson, J.C. *The Origins of St Augustine's, Bristol*, in P McGrath & J Cannon, eds., Essays in Bristol And Gloucestershire History, 1976, 109-26

Fleming, P. & Costello, K. *Discovering Cabot's Bristol*, 1998, 42-56

Groessinger, Crista *The Bristol Misericords and their Sources* in L. Keen, ed. *Bristol in the Middle Ages*, 1997.

Hill, R. *A Letter-book of St Augustine's, Bristol*, Bristol & Gloucestershire Archaeological Society Transactions, 65, 1944, 141-56

Jeayes, I.H. *Abbot Newland's Roll of St Augustine's Abbey*, Bristol & Gloucestershire Archaeological Society Transactions, 14, 1890, 117-30

Leech, R.H. ed. *The Topography of Medieval and Early Modern Bristol*, Bristol Record Society, XLVIII, 1997

Ralph, E. ed. *The Great White Book of Bristol*, Bristol Record Society, 32, 1979, 17-67.

Ralph, E. & Rogan J. *Essays in Cathedral History*, 1991

Sabin, A. ed. *Compotus Rolls of St Augustine's Abbey. Bristol*, Bristol & Gloucestershire Archaeological Society Transactions, 73, 1954-5, 192-207

Sabin, A. *Some Manorial Accounts of St Augustine's Abbey, Bristol*, Bristol Record Society, XXII, 1960

Walker, David *The Cartulary of St Augustine's Abbey, Bristol*, Gloucestershire Record Series, 10, 1998

Worcestre, William *The Topography of Medieval Bristol*, Bristol Record Society, 51, 2000

The Cathedral

Caple, J. *The Bristol Riots of 1831.* Lampeter. 1990. Mellen Press

Barrett, William *The History and Antiquities of the City of Bristol*, 1789. Facsimile Production (Sutton) 1982

Latimer, J. *The Annals of Bristol in the seventeenth century* (Bristol) 1900

Sykes, N. *Church and State in England in the eighteenth century* (Cambridge) 1934

Friends of Bristol Cathedral, ed. E Ralph & J Rogan. *Essays in Cathedral History*

Reports of Friends

Friends' Quarterly Notes

Bettey, J. *Bristol Cathedral : the Rebuilding of the Nave* (Historical Association) 1993

Clarke, B.F.L. *Church Builders of the nineteenth century* (New York) 1969

Cobb, G. *English Cathedrals* (Thames Hudson) London

Ross, J. *Cathedral Church of Bristol* (Gloucester London)1931

Leversage, P. & Taylor, J. *History of Bristol Cathedral.* Clifton (Bristol). 1877

Fletcher, R.J. *A History of Bristol Cathedral* (London) 1932

Romanesque architecture and sculpture

Barrett, W. *The History and Antiquities of Bristol* (1789)

Britton, J. *The History and Antiquities of the Abbey and Cathedral Church of Bristol* (London: Longman) 1830

Burton, J. *Monastic and Religious Orders in Britain 1000-1300* (Cambridge: Cambridge University Press) 1994

Cobb, G. *English Cathedrals: the Forgotten Centuries. Restoration and Change from 1530 to the Present Day* (London: Thames and Hudson) 1980

Dickinson, J.C. 'The Origins of St Augustine's, Bristol' in *Essays in Bristol and Gloucestershire History,* eds. P McGrath & J Cannon (Bristol and Gloucestershire Archaeological Society) 1976

Dickinson, J.C. *The Origins of the Austin Canons and their Introduction in England* (London: SPCK) 1950

Donovan, C. *The Winchester Bible* (London: British Library) 1993

Elliott, J.K. *The Apocryphal New Testament* (Oxford: Clarendon Press) 1993

English Romanesque Art 1066-1200 : Exhibition Catalogue. London, Hayward Gallery 1984 (London: Arts Council of Great Britain) 1984

Gerald of Wales *A Journey through Wales* (Harmondsworth: Penguin) 1978

Godwin, E.S. 'Bristol Cathedral' in *The Archaeological Journal XX* (1863) 38-63

Godwin, E.W. 'An Ancient Coffin Slab in St Philip's Church, Bristol' in *Proceedings of the Archaeological Institute of Great Britain and Ireland* 1851 (London: George Bell) 1853

The Golden Age of Anglo-Saxon Art: Exhibition Catalogue. London, British Museum 1984

(London: British Museum Press) 1984

Hodgson, J. F. 'The Difference of Plans of Churches of Austin Canons and Monks' in *The Archaeological Journal* XLI (1884), XLII (1885) & XLIII (1886)

Jocque, L. & Milis, L. eds. *Liber Ordinis Sancti Victoris Parisiensis* Continuatio Mediaevalis LXI (Turnhout: Brepols) 1984

Kartsonis, A D *Anastasis: The Making of an Image* (Princeton: Princeton University Press) 1986

Kauffmann, C.M. *Romanesque Manuscripts 1066-1190*. A Survey of Manuscripts Illuminated in the British Isles, vol.3 (London: Harvey Miller) 1975

Leonard, G.H. 'Some Norman Remains' in *Proceedings of the Clifton Antiquary Club* VI (1908)

Leversage, P.A. *History of Bristol Cathedral — its antiquities and monuments* 1854

Lyman, C. 'Some Norman Remains of St Augustine's' in *Proceedings of the Clifton Antiquary Club* VI (1905) 59

Massé, H.J.L.J.*The Cathedral Church of Bristol* (London: Bell & Sons) 1901

Mayr-Harting, H *Ottonian Book Illumination* (London: Harvey Miller) 1991

Morgan, E T   *Bristol Cathedral School* (Bristol: Arrowsmith) 1913

Mortet, V   *Recueil des textes Relatifs à l'Histoire de l'Architecture et la Condition des Architectes en France au Moyen Age*. 2 vols. (Paris: Picard) 1911-1929

Muñoz de Miguel, M. 'The Iconography of Christ *Victor* in Anglo-Saxon Art: A New Approach to the Study of the "Harrowing of Hell" Relief in Bristol Cathedral' in L. Keen, *'Almost the Richest City': Bristol in the Middle Ages*. The British Archaeological Association Conference Transactions XIX (London: British Archaeological Association) 1997 75-81

Nicholls, J.F. and Taylor, J. *Bristol, Past and Present*, (Bristol: Arrowsmith) 1881

Norris, J.P. *The Early History and Architecture of Bristol Cathedral* (Bristol) 1888

Paul, R.W. 'The Plan of the Church and Monastery of St Augustine' in *Archaeologia 63* (London: Society of Antiquaries) 1912 231-250

Pevsner, N. *North Somerset and Bristol* 1958, *Shropshire* 1958, *Herefordshire* 1963, The Buildings of England, 46 vols. (London: Penguin Books) 1951–

Prout, J.S. *Picturesque Antiquities of Bristol* 1831

Réau, L. *Iconographie de l'Art Chrétien,* 3 vols. (Paris: Presses Universitaires de France) 1955-1959

Sabin, A. 'The Foundation of the Abbey of St Augustine' in *Transactions of the Bristol and Gloucestershire Archaeological Society* LXXV 1956 35-42

Saxl, F. *English Sculptures of the Twelfth Century* (London: Faber & Faber) 1954

Sculpture and Carved Work in Bristol Cathedral, sketched by E.C. Lavars (Bristol: John Lavars) 1863

Skelton, J. *Etchings of the Antiquities of Bristol, from Original Sketches by the late Hugh O'Neill* 1825

Smith, M.Q. 'The Harrowing of Hell Relief in Bristol Cathedral' in *Transactions of the Bristol and Gloucestershire Archaeological Society* XCIV 1976 101-106

Smith, M.Q. *The Art and Architecture of St Augustine's Abbey*, University of Bristol, History of Art Department, Occasional Paper No.1 1991

Stone, L. *Sculpture in Britain in the Middle Ages* (London: Penguin Books) 1955

Storer, J.K.H. *A History of Bristol Cathedral* 1814

Temple, E. *Anglo-Saxon Manuscripts 900-1066* A Survey of Manuscripts Illuminated in the British Isles vol.2 (London: Harvey Miller) 1976

Thompson, F.H. ed. *Studies in Medieval Sculpture.* Occasional Paper (New Series) III (London: The Society of Antiquaries) 1983

Victoria History of the County of Gloucester, vol.2 (London: Archibald Constable) 1907

Walker, D. ed. *The Cartulary of St Augustine's Abbey, Bristol* (The Bristol and Gloucestershire Archaeological Society) 1998

Worcester, W. *The Itineraries* ed. J Harvey (Oxford: Clarendon Press) 1969

Zarnecki, G. Shobdon, in *Papers given in Memory of Charles Dodwell* 1988

Zarnecki, G. *English Romanesque Sculpture,* 2 vols. (London: Tiranti Limited) 1951 & 1953

Zarnecki, G. *Studies in Romanesque Sculpture* (London: Dorian Press) 1979

Zarnecki, G. *Romanesque Lincoln: the sculpture of the cathedral* (Lincoln: Honeywood) 1988

Dr Oakes would like to acknowledge her debt to the unpublished notes compiled by her former colleague, the late Dr M.Q. Smith, for a book he planned on the architectural history of Bristol Cathedral.

Gothic Architecture

Massé (Bell), H.J.L. *Bristol Cathedral and See* (London) 1910

Great Western Railway *Cathedrals* (London) 1926

Cobb, G. FSA *English Cathedrals — The Forgotten Centuries* (London) 1980

Felton & Harvey *The English Cathedrals* (London) 1950

Harvey, J. *The Gothic World* (London) 1950

Harvey, J. *Gothic England* (London) 1947

Vallance, A. *Greater English Church Screens* (London) 1947

Batsford & Fry *The Cathedrals of England* (London) 1934

Taylor, N. *Looking at Cathedrals* (London) 1968

Quiney, A. *J.L. Pearson* (Yale) 1979

Woodforde, C. *Stained Glass in Somerset* (Oxford) 1946

Roberts, H.E. *Medieval Monasteries and Minsters* (London) 1947

Spence, K. *Cathedrals & Abbeys of England & Wales* (London) 1984

Clarke, B. Rev Canon *Church Builders of the nineteenth century* (London) 1938

Pevsner, N. Sir *An Outline of European Architecture* (Penguin) 1943

Pevsner, N. Sir *The Buildings of England: North Somerset & Bristol* (Penguin) 1958

Fraser, M. *Somerset* [GWR] (London) 1934

Little, Jenner & Gomme *Bristol — an architectural history* (London) 1979

Crick, C. *Victorian Buildings in Bristol* (Bristol) 1975

Winston, R. *Bristol Photographs* (Bristol) 1957

Ross, J. MA (City Librarian) *The Cathedral Church of Bristol* seventh ed. (Gloucester) 1942-3

Burroughs, E.A. Dean DD and R. Paul FSA *Bristol Cathedral* (Bristol) 1924

Godwin, E.W. *The Archaeological Journal* No. 77 (London) 1863

Dammers, A.H. Dean *Bristol Cathedral Guide* (Derby) 1984

Harrison, D.E.W. Dean *Pictorial History of Bristol Cathedral* (London) 1975

Wesley Carr, A. Dean *The Cathedral Illuminated — Son et Lumière*

Bettey, J. Dr FSA *Bristol Cathedral — St Augustine's Abbey* (Bristol) 1996

Bettey, J. Dr FSA *The Suppression of the Religious Houses in Bristol* (Bristol) 1990

Bettey, J. Dr FSA *The Rebuilding of the Nave* (Bristol) 1993

Smith, M.Q. Dr *The Stained Glass of Bristol Cathedral* (Bristol) 1983

Smith, M.Q. Dr *The Art & Architecture of St Augustine's Abbey now Bristol Cathedral* (Bristol) 1991

Smith, M.Q. Dr *The Roof Bosses of Bristol Cathedral* (Bristol) 1979

Holmes, J.G. *A lost architectural feature of Bristol Cathedral* — Proceedings of the Clifton Antiquarian Club (Bristol) 1897

Hipple, R. *Nooks and Crannies* (Yate) 1997

Bell, I. *The Organs of Bristol Cathedral* (Bristol) 1990

Paul, R.W. FSA *The Plan of the Church & Monastery of St Augustine, Bristol* communicated to the Society of Antiquaries (London) 1912

Browne Willis *History* — second edition 1742 (London) 1727

Barrett, W. FSA *History and Antiquaries of the City of Bristol* (London) 1789

Buchanan, A. Prof *Brunel Letters* (University of Bath) 1980

Cawley, D. Rev *Ancient Bells of the Cathedral*

Harrison, S., R.K. Morris and M. Robinson *Pulpitum at Tintern* — Society of Antiquaries (London) 1998

Fletcher, R.J. Canon *A History of Bristol Cathedral* from documents in the possession of the Dean and Chapter (Bristol) 1932

Fitzgerald, M. Canon *The Story of Bristol Cathedral* (Bristol) 1936

Cobb, G. (quotation) *Topographical Excursion, 1634* (London) 1980

Goodhart Rendell, H.S. MusB, MA, FSA, PPRIBA *George Edmund Street* (London) 1953

Latimer, J. *Annals of Bristol* 1887-1902

Britton, J. *The History and Antiquities of the Abbey and Cathedral of Bristol* (London) 1830

Monuments

Annual Reports and Quarterly Notes of the Friends.

Rogan, J. ed. *Cathedral Portraits*

Kemp, B. *English Church Monuments* (London) 1980 Batsford.

Kemp, B. *Church Monuments* (Princes Risborough) 1997 Shire.

Harvey, J. *Gothic World* Batsford — deals with hall churches comprehensively.

Pevsner, N. Sir *Outline of European Architecture* — also addresses the subject, and in his North Somerset & Bristol volume in the *Buildings of England* writes that at Bristol this design appears, perhaps for the first time, with its 'spatial potentialities fully realised'. It became later the leitmotif of late Gothic architecture in Germany. However, the hall church, proper, is a German-Bohemian creation: St Elizabeth's, Marburg (1257–83), the nave of Minden (1267) and other churches in Westphalia.

Wilson, C. *The Gothic Cathedral* — criticises hall churches on account of their symbolic poverty. Though they may make a powerful impression aesthetically, nevertheless they rest upon a utilitarian concept of efficient enclosure of space which reduces their ability to "evoke the heavenly city". There is some theological confusion, which seems to rest upon an over-simplification of the vision of *Civitas Dei*.

Misericords

Groessinger, C. *The World Turned Upside Down* (London) 1997

Owen, D.D.R. ed. *The Romance of Reynard the Fox* (Oxford) 1994

Smith, M.Q. *The Roof Bosses of Bristol Cathedral* 1979 Friends of Bristol Cathedral

Cave, C.J.P *The Roof Bosses of Bristol Cathedral* 1935 Friends of Bristol Cathedral

Hughes, W.W. *Mural Decorations in a Dormitory of the Old Deanery, College Green, Bristol* in Clifton Antiquarian Club V 1900–1903

Stained Glass

This chapter draws heavily upon the work of Dr Michael Q. Smith, especially in his *Stained Glass of Bristol Cathedral*: Friends of Bristol Cathedral 1983. This is an authoritative work and is not likely to be superseded for some time to come

Index

Stourton (Stourhead) 51
Street, George Edmund 19, 60, 105 *seq.*
Stuart, James 116
sub-croft, Norman 105
Sub Sacrist 57
Sutton, Abbot Thomas 31

Temporale 40
Test Act 52
The Builder 108
The Ecclesiologist 60
The Extraordinary Black Book 57
Thomas, J Havard 117-19
Thornborough, Bishop John 41
Tickenham 17
tithes 58
Totterdown 54
Tower, Walter Ernest 137, 139
Towgood, Canon Richard 46
Tractarians 46
Treen Mill 29
Trelawny, Bishop Jonathan 46, 101, 117
Trinity Street 50
Tristram, Professor 112
Tyley, Jabez 117
Tyley, Thomas 117

Under Sacrist 39
Usher 43
Utilitarians 46

Van Somers 44
Vaughan, Sir Charles 49
vaulting, skeleton 92
vestibule, Chapter House 79, 101
Victorines 16
Victorine monastery 78, 120
Visitation 39, 43

Walker, J W & Sons 61
Wapley 19
Warburton, Dean 50
Warwick, Richard of 19
Weare 17
Wells Cathedral 21, 30
Wells, Dean of 21, 88
Westfield, Bishop Thomas 44
Westmacott, Richard 117
Weston-super-mare 17

Wetherell, Sir Charles 54
Whall, Christopher 140
White, Thomas 103
Whitefriars screen 103
William of Rical 27
William of Saltmarsh 19
William of Worcester 15, 48, 53
William the Geometer 89
William, Prince of Orange 46
Winkles 81
Winkworth, Catherine 118, 119
Woore 137
Wotton-under-Edge 19
Wraxall 17
Wright, Bishop Robert 41, 136

Young, Sir John and Lady 48